"NOAH'S ARKITECTURE"

A Study of
Dickens's Mythology

By Bert G. Hornback

OHIO UNIVERSITY PRESS
ATHENS, OHIO
1972

© 1972 by Bert G. Hornback
Library of Congress Catalog Card Number 70-181681
ISBN 8214-0100-9
Printed in the United States of America by
Oberlin Printing Co.

FOR ANN AND GUY

TED AND TRISH

CONTENTS

A Note on References and Editions

Quotations from Dickens's novels throughout are from *The New Oxford Illustrated Dickens* (London, 1947-1958), and their citations appear parenthetically in my text. References to other of Dickens's writings are given in footnotes.

The following abbreviations are used throughout in referring to the novels:

PP	*The Pickwick Papers*
OT	*Oliver Twist*
NN	*Nicholas Nickleby*
OCS	*The Old Curiosity Shop*
BR	*Barnaby Rudge*
MHC	*Master Humphrey's Clock*
MC	*Martin Chuzzlewit*
D&S	*Dombey and Son*
DC	*David Copperfield*
BH	*Bleak House*
LD	*Little Dorrit*
HT	*Hard Times*
TTC	*A Tale of Two Cities*
GE	*Great Expectations*
OMF	*Our Mutual Friend*
ED	*Edwin Drood*
CS	*Christmas Stories*

ACKNOWLEDGMENTS

I WISH TO EXPRESS MY APPRECIATION TO PROFESSOR JOSEPH M. Duffy of the University of Notre Dame, with whom I first studied Dickens; to my aunt, Mrs. Dorothy Borrone Greer, who gave me my first set of Dickens's novels; to Professors Warner G. Rice and Robert H. Super of the University of Michigan, and Professor Arthur J. Carr of Williams College, who first encouraged me in my lectures on Dickens; to Professors Donald Hall, Ejner J. Jensen, and John W. Wright of the University of Michigan, who have talked and listened and argued with me about Dickens for the last several years; to Professor J. Hillis Miller of the Johns Hopkins University, whose *Charles Dickens: The World of His Novels* is the sourcebook for so many of my ideas; to Professor Robert J. Heaman of Wilkes College, who has shared many hours and numerous ideas with me; to Professor John Whitley of the University of Sussex, England; to the many students who have read Dickens with me and helped me to understand him; to Mr. Dale Simmerman, Mr. James Hennerty, Miss Nancy Wicker, and Miss Miriam Murchie; to Mrs. Susan Schulman; to Mr. Paddy Egan of Dublin, who drew me many pints of Guinness during the summer that I actually wrote most of this; and to the hundred or so people a year who come to Dickens's birthday party at my home, to help me celebrate him.

The *David Copperfield* chapter of this book originally appeared in a somewhat different form as "Frustration and Resolution in *David Copperfield*," in *Studies in English Literature*, 8(Autumn 1968): 652-67. Parts of chapters 1, 4, and 7 were published originally in "Dickens's Argument with the Law," in *Dimensions* 1(October 1970): 8-15.

My title comes from one of the titles Dickens ordered for his dummy library. *Noah's Arkitecture* was a two-volume study there. The pun in "Arkitecture" is as important as Noah himself, for Dickens. Every man's house is his ark, and in Dickens's world the architectural order of civilization is failing.

NOAH'S ARKITECTURE

It rained hard all the way, and I thought that life was sloppier than I had expected to find it.
CHARLES DICKENS

One does not survive a cataclysm easily.
SHIRLEY JACKSON

INTRODUCTION

W ALLACE STEVENS ONCE WROTE, CASUALLY, THAT "IMAGI-
nation and society are inseparable."[1] What I propose in
this book is an examination of that inseparableness in the art of
Charles Dickens, and an exploration of the vision of the world he
creates from it. Dickens's vision is double: it is realistic, though
often in an exaggerated way, as a picture of the world as it is;
and it is mythic as an interpretation of this world in a universal
context. The inseparableness of the imagination and the society
in which it lives makes it impossible to say that Dickens the realist is Dickens the social critic, and Dickens the myth-maker is
Dickens the artist. The two are one. In *David Copperfield* David
speaks of "the blending of experience and imagination" as the
activity of his mind when he is engaged in writing fiction (DC,
p. 665). What this "blending" accomplishes is the making of
the double vision into one vision; and we can say, then, with some
sureness, that the realistic and the mythic elements of Dickens's
novels make one fiction—that they are as inseparable as the artist's mind and the matter it works with.

We know what Victorian society and civilization were like,
and what Dickens's critical responses to it were. He attacked its
schools, its workhouses, its failures to provide for the poor and

---

1. *The Necessary Angel* (New York, 1965), p. 28.

1

the sick. He attacked institutionalized religion and the institutions of law and government. Etc., etc. After *David Copperfield* the nature of Dickens's argument with his world changes somewhat. There are still critical representations of individual evils, like M'Choakumchild's school in *Hard Times* and the parish unions in *Our Mutual Friend*; but there are also larger attacks upon the nature of society and civilization itself. In his attack on chancery in *Bleak House* he attacks the institution of the law as it represents the primary ordering force in our civilized world. In *Little Dorrit*, similarly, he represents the whole idea of government in the Circumlocution Office. *Hard Times* is a condemnation of industrialism as a way of life. In each of these novels the primary revolutionary is Dickens. In *A Tale of Two Cities* he turns back to the time of revolution, and explores his present world under the guise of history. From so close and particular a perspective he must see and feel the violence of the revolution—real now, not symbolic—and he is shocked and appalled. But he learns something important in this novel. By examining his revolution as he does, he discovers the center and source of the evil in his world, and the critical subject matter of his last two complete novels. What is wrong with society, for Dickens, is the idea of class; and both *Great Expectations* and *Our Mutual Friend* are arguments against the class society. To be "civilized," as Mortimer Lightwood says at the end of *Our Mutual Friend*, is to engage in "eating one another" (OMF, p. 816), which is a lovely habit, it seems, of the class society.

Dickens's criticism of society is presented in the world of his novels, in his characters and the way they live, and where they live. Society lives in a physically described real world in Dickens's novels, and that physical world matches the evil of inhabiting society with its own chaos. This is true in all of the novels, from *Pickwick Papers* through *Our Mutual Friend*. In the early books this matching seems to be more taken for granted than symbolic, as Dickens focuses his critical attention on particular institutional evils and individual character flaws. He often uses the tumbling down of houses, the "wilderness," and the general decay of the world around to establish critical atmosphere; but in the novels through *Dombey and Son* he does not connect this failure of order directly with society as he does in the later novels. Beginning in *David Copperfield*, or perhaps in *Bleak House*, the critical focus turns, and the chaotic physical environment in which we live is seen more and more as a direct result of the social and political environment which we have created, calling it "civilization." Even in the first seven novels the statement of chaos is so pervasive that, despite the lack of any positively asserted cause-and-effect relationship between general social disorder and the world's physical decay, we sense the connection between the two. Dickens is always and essentially an environmentalist, except when he blinds himself—out of fear or a desperate need for reassurance—to the world he has created and fabricates unreal creatures like Oliver Twist, whose language, manners, values, and ideas all betray his silver-spooned irrelevance to his world.

Perhaps the most basic theme in all Dickens's writings is "the initiation of children into the ways of life" (OCS, p. 6). In the early novels his young heroes and heroines confront the individual and particular evils of the world as they grow up, and if those evils are small enough the good people triumph over them. When the evils are found to be too large—when they seem at last to pervade the whole world—the good people retreat, gathering about themselves other good people to make something like an alternate world, a little pocket of love where they can live happily ever after. Mr. Pickwick—he is new to the ways of the world, though not a young man—is the first of these heroes, and his adventures make the pattern. Dickens tries to call Mr. Pickwick's defeat in the large world a victory, and his retreat is represented as a going forth, with marriages and children ending the whole affair. What Dickens learns in *Pickwick Papers*—from his critical vision, it seems—causes him to introduce two safety devices into his story pattern in *Oliver Twist*. One is the benevolent man, who is only peripherally involved in the world of the novel, and who thus can intervene to save the hero or heroine in any extreme danger; the other is the "principle of Good," a proof against the world with which Dickens invests the hero.

Mr. Pickwick was the first benevolent gentleman, but he made the mistake of getting too far into the world, where his benevolence proved ineffective. Later benevolent gentlemen keep their distance from the world of experience, and act accordingly. They are all bachelors, and all wealthy: Mr. Brownlow in *Oliver Twist*, the Cheeryble brothers in *Nicholas Nickleby*, the Single Gentleman (Master Humphrey) in *The Old Curiosity Shop*, and Mr. Jarndyce in *Bleak House*. Old Martin assumes the role of the benevolent gentleman at the end of *Martin Chuzzlewit*, and Captain Cuttle does so in a minor way in *Dombey and Son*. In their maidenly retreats Miss Betsey Trotwood in *David Copperfield* and Miss Havisham in *Great Expectations* are also versions of the benevolent character. Magwitch is also a benevolent gentleman of sorts when he returns to make Pip's fortune; he is perhaps a combination of Mr. Brownlow and Fagin.

Oliver himself is the original "principle of Good surviving through every adverse circumstance, and triumphing at last."[2] There are various later characters who share this role with him, though none of them suffers from the unreality which his goodness makes for him. Little Nell in *The Old Curiosity Shop* is perhaps the worst of the others in her unnatural goodness; the sweetness of Florence Dombey and the essential piety of Sissy Jupe in *Hard Times* are similar. Amy Dorrit and Lizze Hexam in *Our Mutual Friend* have the same kind of protection that Oliver has, but Dickens salvages them as characters. Esther Summerson in *Bleak House* and David Copperfield are also in some

---

2. *Oliver Twist*, preface of 1841.

way "principle of Good" characters, though it may be more useful to speak of them as embodying a "principle of Love" instead, and representing thus Dickens's alternative to the "principle of Good"—and even his substitute for benevolence as well—as they learn through love to work in the world for change.[3] What ties all of these characters together is their embodiment of substantial and unassailable goodness, and their consequent invulnerableness to any evil influence. They are all secularly miraculous immaculate conceptions, except for Esther and David: David's miracle is alleged in terms of the natural superstition attached to being "born with a caul" (DC, p. 1), and Esther's birth is illegitimate. Most of these "good" characters do not develop or change, and in their stasis, their immutability, they demonstrate their own inadequacy as solutions to the problem of evil, for the world in which they stand still is a world dissolving into ruin about them, and in urgent need of active rebuilding.

Dickens's world is a world of change; and the opposing forces are growth in his characters and decay in civilization. In the early novels the degeneration often overwhelms him, and he takes his characters away into their retreats to save them. In the later novels, though his vision of the chaos and disorder gets much darker, his conclusion is more consistently optimistic and heroic. There seems to be more opportunity for changing things for the better in the later novels. There are more people who have a "power of doing good" (DC, p. 843; OMF, p. 680), and thus making a new beginning out of, and in the midst of, all that has gone wrong. His thesis in these novels is "that you can't shut out the world; that you are in it, to be of it . . . and that you must

---

3. Almost all of the "principle of Good" characters are girls, and most of Dickens's heroes are young men who must overcome the example of this goodness in order to fulfill themselves. Dickens's main concern is with metaphysics, not morality. The defense of goodness is given to people whose selves are not strong enough to stand up against the world, and sometimes these weak people almost seduce Dickens's young men out of themselves with their piety.

mingle with it, and make the best of it, and make the best of yourself into the bargain."[4]

To make the best of this world means to find and make new beginnings in it, and these new beginnings are the primary focus of this book. I am concerned to explore Dickens's mythology and to relate it to the stories he tells as he elaborates it. Dickens's mythology is one of new beginnings, a Genesis mythology. The recurring mythic symbols are the days of the Creation, Eden, the Flood, Noah's Ark, and the tower of Babel. These Genesis symbols create a mythic time-setting for the novels in which the movement of the world of change takes place. Movement in the real world of time—the few years of any novel's action—is too slight to be discerned, but change in the foreshortened world of mythic time can be immense. The movement varies: sometimes it is from the coming of the Flood through the retreat into the Ark toward a landing on Mount Ararat. Sometimes the end of the novel is like "the Day of Judgment." Often there is an attempt to return to Eden, though after the first novels Eden usually turns out to be either a "ruined garden," a "wilderness" like the rest of the world, or a heaven and thus out of this world and this life altogether. These various references are generally mixed; in almost every novel Dickens uses the whole set of Genesis symbols to create the myth. What he argues through this mythic dimension is our ability to survive in the real world in which we actually live, and the possibility of our making a new beginning in it. Sometimes, particularly in the early novels, the conclusions Dickens reaches in his mythology are much more realistic than those with which he ends his stories. In the later novels, the myth and the story resolve as one.

In the myth, the chaos of our world is like that which existed before God created order, particularly the order of the third day, which separated the land from the waters. Thus the world is

---

4. Dickens to Wilkie Collins, 6 September 1858.

6

filled with mud, and ooze, and slime. Eden was a perfectly ordered place once; but now, after Adam's fall, it is a "labyrinth," a "maze," a "wilderness," a "bleak place overgrown with nettles." Things get so bad the Flood comes, to destroy it all; and Noah attempts to ride it out on the Ark, and begin the world again. In the early novels this myth is elaborated as a sort of descant over the story. In several of these novels—those which end in the hero's retreat—it underlines the inadequacy of Dickens's solution to the problem he has found in the chaos. Later, the burden of the myth and the development of the story parallel each other, and the conclusion of the story fulfills the myth. In both *Great Expectations* and *Our Mutual Friend* the mythic dimension becomes one with that of the action, and the myth is directly realized in the story. In *Great Expectations* Pip becomes a new Adam, and learns to live successfully by hard work in the postlapsarian world. In *Our Mutual Friend* various characters are drowned or almost drowned, as the myth becomes real. The chaos now is not that of the Flood, but the real river Thames; the only Ark is a toy Ark that little Johnny has, and every man must find his own salvation.

David Copperfield seems very much the central novel in Dickens's development. David is his "favorite child," his autobiographical self in part. What is most important is that David is a novelist, an artist. Blending his experience and imagination, David finds the truth which is the product of the two. In David's voice Dickens finds for the first time a sound, workable resolution of myth and story. David takes control of the world by understanding it with his imagination; and what he achieves is a "power of doing good" (DC, p. 60). In terms of the myth, David is Dickens's first successful Noah, and "All Creation" takes the name of Copperfield in his comprehension of it.

In tracing Dickens's mythology from its first formulations in the simple world which Mr. Pickwick supposes to exist through to its terrible realization in the world of *Our Mutual Friend*

I hope to elucidate what seem to me his most important themes, to represent the seriousness of his philosophy of love, and to uncover for the interested reader another rich and enriching dimension of Dickens's inexhaustible fiction.

1

THE EARLY NOVELS

I

THE FIRST FOUR OF DICKENS'S NOVELS, FROM *Pickwick Papers* through *The Old Curiosity Shop*, form a unit of sorts, though to be sure they are four very different novels, each with its own character and charm, and each with its own thesis or plan for solving the world which it discovers and represents. For Dickens's career, *Pickwick Papers* is perhaps the most interesting.

Mr. Pickwick is Dickens's first explorer. He is the first of a dozen "benevolent" men in Dickens's world, and he is the first version of David Copperfield, the young novelist who sets out to comprehend the world. The full title of the later novel is *The Personal History, Adventures, Experience, and Observation of David Copperfield the Younger*. In the opening pages of *Pickwick Papers* we discover that Mr. Pickwick proposes "extending his travels, and consequently enlarging his sphere of observation, to the advancement of knowledge, and the diffusion of learning." He will forward to the Pickwick Club "accounts of their journeys and investigations, of their observations of character and manners, and of the whole of their adventures" (PP, pp. 1-2). David is an artist; Mr. Pickwick is a note taker and letter writer. As an artist, David has a "power of doing good" (DC, p. 843); the best Mr. Pickwick can say for himself at the end of his career is, "If I have done but little good, I trust I have done less harm" (PP, p. 797). He only hopes his "adventures" will be "a source of amusing and pleasant recollection" to him in his retirement; David is told that his novels are read "with delight, with entertainment, with instruction" (DC, p. 872).

At the beginning of his novel, the innocent Mr. Pickwick's gentlemanly observations of the world seem to have been confined to "Speculations on the Source of the Hampstead Ponds, with some Observations on the Theory of Tittlebats" (PP, p. 1). But he is an "observer of human nature" (PP, p. 11), and he sets out with "the desire to benefit the human race" (PP, p. 4). He finds in London an "opportunity of contemplating human nature in all the numerous phases it exhibits" (PP, p. 150), and takes advantage of it. He joins the famous drinking party at the Magpie and Stump because he "could not resist so tempting an opportunity of studying human nature" (PP, p. 276). The climax of his experience of the world and human nature comes at his arrest in chapter 40, which "Introduces Mr. Pickwick to a New and not Uninteresting Scene in the Great Drama of Life" (PP, p. 560). This is all comedy, of course, but serious comedy because it is a comedy of disillusionment,, frustration, and failure. Even the title of the novel tells us this: these are *The Posthumous Papers of the Pickwick Club*. We are informed at the outset that "general benevolence was one of the leading features of the Pickwickian theory" (PP, p. 16), and what the novel tests is the efficacy of this theory in practice in the world. Twice Mr. Pickwick is referred to as a "philosopher," once by Jingle (PP, p. 11), and once by the whimsical narrator (PP, p. 131). But this is at least in part a serious description of what the old gentleman sees as his role of life, and it is this seriousness that makes the novel so much more for us as readers than just rollicking picaresque comedy. Mr. Pickwick lives by his "theory" of "benevolence"; and in his innocent faith in that theory, he meets the world with a "countenance glow[ing] with an expression of universal philanthropy" (PP, p. 16).

For a world as large, complex, and chaotic as the world Dickens saw, even at the beginning of his career, this philosophy is at best naïve and simpleminded. Indeed, Dickens seems to know this: through the first half of the novel one of the continuing jokes is the use of "benevolence" as a comic euphemism for drunkenness. Mr. Pickwick returns drunk from the tavern to Dingley Dell, "shaking his head from side to side, and producing a constant succession of the blandest and most benevolent smiles without being moved thereunto by any discernible cause or pretense whatsoever" (PP, p. 99). On the hunting expedition, a "constant succession of glasses [of punch] produced considerable effect upon Mr. Pickwick; his countenance beamed with the most sunny smiles, laughter played around his lips, and good-humoured merriment twinkled in his eyes" (PP, p. 257). In the affair of honor with Dr. Slammer, Mr. Pickwick's righteous wrath is calmed by "the virtues of a bumper" applied to his mouth; soon "the brandy and water had done its work; the amiable countenance of Mr. Pickwick was fast recovering its customary expression" (PP, pp. 43-44)—the smile called "benevolence."

Benevolence meets its match and more in the law; and the world organized by this corrupt and corrupting institution overcomes the minor forces of simple benevolence. Mr. Pickwick's first encounter with the law is at the White Hart Inn in London; the incident is that of Jingle's running away with Miss Wardle, and the law is represented by Mr. Perker, who is a man of the world. "We are both men of the world," Perker says to Jingle, the confidence man; and he continues, speaking of Mr. Pickwick and Mr. Wardle, "and *we* know very well that our friends here are not" (PP, p. 129). Mr. Pickwick comes out of this crisis reasonably well. Perker bribes Jingle, Mr. Wardle takes Miss Wardle home to Dingley Dell, and Mr. Pickwick resumes his benevolent manner, very much unenlightened by the whole affair. His next meeting with the law, however, is more serious, and again, it is over a question of marriage. Chapter 18 introduces the central plot-conflict of the novel, the lawsuit of "Bardell against Pickwick," which occupies then the next thirty chapters (there are fifty-seven in all), until Mr. Pickwick is released from prison at the end of chapter 47.

Sam Weller describes Mr. Pickwick's benevolent character once: "I never heard, mind you, nor read of in story-books, nor see in picters, any angel in tights and gaiters—not even in spectacles, as I can remember . . . he's a reg'lar thoroughbred angel for all that" (PP, p. 642). Mr. Pickwick is at this time new to imprisonment in the Fleet; and immediately after this speech (to Job Trotter) Sam takes him on a tour of the prison. What the innocent, angelic Mr. Pickwick sees is a terrible microcosmic picture of the world—the large world, imprisoned in "squalor" and "turmoil" and "noise," the "whole place . . . restless and troubled; and the people . . . crowding, and flitting to and fro, like the shadows in an uneasy dream" (PP, p. 645). This description is much like that which concludes *Little Dorrit*; but Amy and Arthur Clennam "[go] quietly down into the roaring streets," to live and work there; whereas Mr. Pickwick can only retreat from the experience: " 'I have seen enough,' said Mr. Pickwick, as he threw himself into a chair in his little apartment. 'My head aches with these scenes, and my heart too. Henceforth I will be a prisoner in my own room' " (PP, p. 645).

From this crisis to the end of the novel takes but little space. Mr. Pickwick has gone to prison standing, as Sam says, on "principle" (PP, p. 489). He refuses to pay the damages awarded unjustly by the court. But though Mr. Pickwick is in prison, he is never really imprisoned—just as, in Dickens's next novel, Oliver Twist is never really in danger of becoming a true member of Fagin's gang. Oliver has his shield of "goodness" to protect him from evil; Mr. Pickwick has his money. And after his discovery of the horror of the prison—a horror which benevolence cannot correct or undo—he quietly agrees to pay costs to Dodson and Fogg, and thus release himself and Mrs. Bardell. As he leaves the Fleet, he leaves behind him a record of mercy and benevolence: "In all the crowd of wan, emaciated faces, he saw not one which was not the happier for his sympathy and charity" (PP, p. 666). Still, they are wan and emaciated, and they remain in prison; benevolence has not been able to change the world, to remake it to correspond to Mr. Pickwick's original innocent conception of it. Earlier, in his first encounter with corruption in politics, he cried in astonishment, "Can such things be!" (PP, p. 166). Now his "adventures" and "observations" leave him disillusioned, and he retires. He surrounds himself with his friends, and is seen "retiring to some quiet pretty neighborhood in the vicinity of London. . . . trusting that I may yet live to spend many quiet years in peaceful retirement." From "this little retreat" he announces the "dissolution" of the Pickwick Club, and makes a speech:

"I shall never regret having devoted the greater part of two years to mixing with different varieties and shades of human character: frivolous as my persuit of novelty may have appeared to many. Nearly the whole of my previous life having been devoted to business and the pursuit of wealth, numerous scenes of which I had no previous conception have dawned upon me—I hope to the enlargement of my mind, and the improvement of my understanding. If I have done but little good, I trust I have done less harm, and that none of my adventures will be other than a source of amusing and pleasant recollection to me in the decline of life. God bless all!" (PP, pp. 796-97)

Pickwick Papers closes, then, with a blissful evening scene. Everyone loves and honors Mr. Pickwick. Sam Weller and Mary are married with his blessing, and have "two sturdy boys"; the Snodgrasses, the Winkles, and the Trundles make "numerous applications" to him, "to act as godfather to their offspring" (PP, p. 801). The Pickwickian world is happy, and these marriages and their children are the first instance of Dickens's standard metaphor for the promise of a better future. But behind this peaceful scene and its promise is the weight of the world which Mr. Pickwick has left behind. In his disillusionment and subsequent retirement is the seed of Dickens's career as a serious novelist. Never again is there such innocence or innocent comedy as there was at the beginning of *Pickwick Papers.* The rest of Dickens's career is spent dealing with the world which Mr. Pickwick quit, honored and blessed for his goodness, but in the last analysis defeated.

2

Oliver Twist is generally so much a different novel from *Pickwick Papers* that it may seem strange to begin by pointing out the things that tie them together. The ties are ties of transition; they are what take Dickens from the one to the other. Until we see this, we will not see the important relationship between the two. First of all, Oliver doesn't go to jail, as Mr. Pickwick did. And he is not disillusioned, as Mr. Pickwick was. He remains an innocent throughout—indeed, as Dickens described him in the preface to the 1841 edition, "the principle of Good surviving through every adverse circumstance, and triumphing at last." With what one might almost assume was the energy of his own innocence, Dickens introduced the innocent Mr. Pickwick to the world with no support other than his wealth, his good intentions, and a trust in the general efficacy of personal benevolence. Learning from Mr. Pickwick's experience, Dickens equips the world of *Oliver Twist* with a force larger and stronger than Mr. Pickwick's unsure and overextended benevolence: a "principle of Good," watched over by "that Being whose code is Mercy, and whose great attribute is Benevolence" (OT, p. 415). Oliver is the human embodiment of this "principle of Good," and lives thus a charmed and fabular life. In the end, we are told, he and his are "truly happy" (OT, p. 415).

Oliver Twist is a sentimental novel in its conception and in its thesis. In its dramatic execution, however, it is by and large free from sentimentalism. At least it is so charged with fine examples of Dickens's realistic and surrealistic art that we are not prejudiced by the occasions of sentimentalism. Even from the first chapter, there is never any sense in *Oliver Twist* that this is an innocent world. Humor and comedy are mixed in with the great seriousness; but the comedy is there by way of relief, and the narrative humor only tells us Dickens's determination from the beginning for Oliver's "surviving through every circumstance, and triumphing at last." In the opening paragraph Dickens refers to the yet-unnamed Oliver as an "item of mortality," and in each of the next two paragraphs exercises his wit on the precariousness of Oliver's youthful life. These threats are comic for us, else "it is somewhat more than probable that these memoirs would never have appeared" (OT, p. 1), but they are terribly serious for Oliver. At the climax of the first dramatic sequence of the novel he is threatened again, by "the gentleman in the white waistcoat": "That boy will be hung," he says, three times over—and "nobody controverted the prophetic gentleman's opinion" (OT, p. 13).

The threat of hanging follows Oliver throughout the novel. And though Dickens has made clear to us his determination to save him, that never makes the threat any less real to Oliver, or the sense of impending doom any less impressive for us. Through its constant suggestion, hanging becomes the one great expectation of the novel. No less than forty-eight times hanging is referred to, or suggested: from that first warning about Oliver's future prospects, to Mr. Fang's addressing him as "young gallows" (OT, p. 69), to Bill Sikes's "dumb show" of hanging (OT, p. 87), to Fagin's "drawing a rather disagreeable picture of the discomforts of hanging" for Oliver (OT, p. 127), to the tinker's attempt at Mrs. Maylie's "to restore Oliver, lest he should die before he could be hanged" (OT, p. 210), to Monks's admission that he would have dragged Oliver "to the very gallows-foot" if he could (OT, p. 397). What this fantastic profusion of imagery and suggestion does to us, as readers, is indirectly explained by Nancy in her conversation with Mr. Brownlow just before her death:

> "Horrible thoughts of death . . . have been upon me all day. I was reading a book to-night, to wile the times away, and the same things came into the print."
> "Imagination," said the gentleman, soothing her.
> "No imagination," replied the girl in a hoarse voice. "I'll swear I saw 'coffin' written in every page in the book in large black letters." (OT, p. 350)

Dickens gives us the same sense in reading *Oliver Twist* that Nancy has reading her book; we are given "thoughts of death" and images of "hanging" on every page we read. Our fears—and Oliver's—are finally released when Bill Sikes and Fagin are hanged, and Oliver is then safe.

The life of *Oliver Twist* exists on this dramatic and psychological level. There is another dimension to the novel, however, and it must also be considered, both because it explains the weaknesses in Dickens's dramatic conception and because it was itself important to Dickens in the creation of the novel. This is the matter of the fable, and the faith that supports it. We see it directly for the first time in the narrative representation of Fagin's questionably motivated attempt to transform Oliver into a criminal:

> In short, the wily old Jew had the boy in his toils. Having prepared his mind, by solitude and gloom, to prefer any society to the companionship of his sad thoughts in such a dreary place, he was now slowly instilling into his soul the poison which he hoped would blacken it, and change its hue forever. (OT, p. 134)

Opposing this influence, however, is Oliver's fabular birthright of goodness, suggested first in Mr. Brownlow's response to Oliver's face (OT, p. 70), and then reinforced in Oliver's innocent response to his mother's "beautiful, mild face" (OT, p. 79). This goodness keeps him from harm: "he was not like other boys in the same circumstances," says Fagin, and Monks answers, "Curse him, no! . . . or he would have been a thief, long ago" (OT, p. 193). Nancy says, "The sight of him turns me against myself, and all of you" (OT, p. 189); and later Mr. Brownlow tells Monks, piously, that "the sight of the persecuted child has turned vice itself, and given it the courage and almost the attributes of virtue" (OT, p. 379).

Oliver's true nature (what Dickens calls the "true self" in *Dombey and Son* [D&S, pp. 477, 839]) is good, or goodness; and Dickens's postulate for this novel is that good triumphs. In a way the good world that Oliver finds—with Mr. Brownlow, with the Maylies—is like Mr. Pickwick's world at the end of his novel, a retreat. Mr. Brownlow is in fact Dickens's new Mr. Pickwick, another benevolent bachelor; but he is stronger than Mr. Pickwick, more carefully aware of the world, and more removed from it—more like Mr. Jarndyce in *Bleak House*, finally, than Mr. Pickwick. The difference between *Oliver Twist* and *Pickwick Papers* is that Mr. Pickwick could not manage the evil of the large world and retreated from it; here the story is not that of the benevolent gentleman and his disillusionment, but rather the story of a boy who lives *in* the evil world and finds as his reward the goodness which continues to exist in spite of evil. That evil pervades the world Dickens now accepts; but he insists that goodness can survive, albeit in almost desperate retreat from that evil. In the end, Mr. Brownlow "link[s] together a little society" (OT, p. 412) by adopting Oliver. Rose and Harry are married, and raise children, and, we are told, they are all "truly happy" (OT, p. 415).

This happiness—come as it has through the trials of "adversity"—is based upon the Christian concept of heavenly reward. From our experience of Dickens's later works, particularly the

description of Betsey Trotwood's "little piece of green" in front
of her house at Dover, the "sacred precincts," or "hallowed
green," or "immaculate spot" which she protects, it should become clear to us that the wonderful house with the "large garden" to which Mr. Pickwick retires, and which he proposes to
"consecrate" with a blessed marriage, is really a new Eden; and
that much like Miss Betsey, so Mr. Pickwick is not just in retreat
from the world, but is trying to start it over again—right. Thus
Mr. Pickwick's attempt to create a new and innocent world, to
reestablish a simple Eden, is the key for Dickens's resort to
Christian mythology in *Oliver Twist*. What the mythology of
Oliver Twist does is pretend to prove the Christian faith in heav-
en, by means of its local institution, finally, here on earth.

Very early in the novel, the first time he is taken to Mr. Brownlow's, Oliver talks of heaven, and of his mother being happy
there (OT, p. 77). Later, Oliver, whose chances for learning
either Christian faith or piety in his nine years have been almost
nil, cries out in moral terror to Sikes, "Oh! for God's sake let me
go! . . . For the love of all the bright Angels that rest in Heaven,
have mercy upon me" (OT, p. 162). This kind of earnestly pious
invocation is new to Dickens here; it does not appear at all in
Pickwick Papers. (I am not suggesting that such sentiments,
spoken seriously, would have been unusual in the nineteenth
century, but simply that such sentiments are new here for Dickens's fiction.)

There are other instances of this protestation of faith in the
novel. When Rose Maylie recovers from her illness, it is announced by Dr. Losberne as God's will: "As He is good and
merciful, she will live to bless us all, for years to come" (OT,
p. 297). When Nancy tells Rose of herself, she cries, "Thank
Heaven upon your knees, dear lady . . . that you had friends to
care for and keep you in your childhood" (OT, p. 302)—a combination of Christian piety and environmental sociology. When
Nancy dies, she holds Rose's white handkerchief "towards Heav-

en," and breathes "one prayer for mercy to her Maker" (OT, p. 362). Oliver wants to pray with Fagin in Newgate (OT, p. 411). And Mrs. Maylie explains to Oliver concerning Rose's sickness "that it is not always the youngest and best who are spared to those who love them; but this should give us comfort in our sorrow; for Heaven is just; and such things teach us, impressively, that there is a brighter world than this. . . . God's will be done" (OT, p. 242). In the end, "the two orphans, tried by adversity," give "fervent thanks to Him who had protected and preserved them," and are "truly happy" (OT, p. 415). This happiness is the happiness of heaven, on earth; or, more precisely, it is the happiness which guarantees and proves emblematically that there is "a brighter world" to come. For "this happiness can never be attained," Dickens says in closing *Oliver Twist*, "without strong affection and humanity of heart, and gratitude to that Being whose code is Mercy, and whose greatest attribute is Benevolence to all things that breathe" (OT, p. 415).

But this happiness is not of this world, and thus it is neither convincing nor satisfying. When Rose is first introduced she is presented as other-worldly, and she remains so throughout the novel. She is "at that age, when, if ever angels be for God's good purposes enthroned in mortal forms, they may be . . . supposed to abide in such as hers." She is "so mild and gentle; so pure and beautiful; that earth seemed not her element, nor its rough creatures her fit companions" (OT, p. 212). When Oliver has recovered from his wound, he and Rose and Mrs. Maylie go together to a cottage in the country, which is just so far removed from the real world and this life as Rose and Oliver deserve: "It was a happy time. The days were peaceful and serene; the nights brought with them neither fear nor care; no languishing in a wretched prison, or associating with wretched men; nothing but pleasant and happy thoughts" (OT, p. 238). Dickens pretends that this secluded life is bliss. But all he has done is retreat from prisons and wretched men; he has neither abolished the prisons nor saved the men by giving Oliver and Rose such a happy time. He must have known, somewhere inside his mind, that this kind of retreat was wrong. For though he talks of "pleasant and happy thoughts," he images death in his description of the place:

> It was a lovely spot to which they repaired. . . . Hard by, was a little churchyard; not crowded with tall unsightly grave-stones, but full of humble mounds, covered with fresh turf and moss; beneath which, the old people of the village lay at rest. (OT, p. 238)

This retreat matches that to which all the good people retire at the end of the novel. And there, too, what Dickens calls "happiness" is presented with a curious morbidity: Oliver's and Rose's "love for one another" is expressed in their "passing whole hours together in picturing the friends whom they had so sadly lost" (OT, p. 415).

The real world is full of "squalid crowds, and . . . noise and brawling" (OT, p. 238), and Dickens is at this point unable to deal with it. Mr. Pickwick had to retire to escape from it; Oliver and his friends retreat, and Dickens hoists a "lonely in the faith" banner, arguing their Christian love—their "strong affection" for each other and their general "humanity of heart"—as justification for calling their defeat another victory.[1] Dickens will never give up on "strong affection and humanity of heart" as the virtues necessary for the salvation of this world. Later in his career, however, he becomes more and more concerned with just this world, and he forsakes the old orthodox religious mythology

---

1. Perhaps *Oliver Twist* is a "posthumous" novel, just as *Pickwick Papers* is more correctly *The Posthumous Papers of The Pickwick Club*; perhaps this is the sense or meaning of the morbidity with which this second novel closes. It is also possible that the reason Dickens has Fagin executed—and the reason that chapter 52 is so strongly written—is that he was unwilling to accept Fagin's den as a little pocket of love that actually worked in the real London world. There is certainly more pleasure, more vitality, more "strong affection and humanity of heart" even, in Fagin's world than there is elsewhere in the novel. But Dickens was not ready yet to understand life in any serious way independent of conventional good and evil, and thus Fagin had to die.

which so informs this novel, and develops in its place a natural
—and naturalized—descriptive mythology of his own.

3

Nicholas Nickleby is Dickens's next novel, and, like *Oliver
Twist*, it is a mixture of success and failure. If one looks at it
simply, it is a long, rambling tale of young Nicholas's adventures, held together more by Nicholas himself and the sequence
of page numbers than by any organic form or unity of design.
It is a highly rhetorical novel, melodramatically and unnaturally
so, full of speech-making and posturing. It almost seems as
though, after his successes as a storyteller in *Pickwick Papers* and
Oliver Twist, Dickens has regressed and is not sure even how to
write a novel now—let alone how to organize the world.

It may be the pressure of trying to organize the world and to
comprehend it imaginatively and philosophically that distracts
Dickens in this novel from the easy, true vitality which characterizes most of his other works. The emotional charge of his rhetoric
and that of his characters reveals his unsureness, as does his remarkable preoccupation with his thesis, which is the worth of
the "heart," or love; references to "heart" and "hearts" appear
nearly two hundred times in the novel.

Nicholas Nickleby is a thesis novel more than any other kind,
and the thesis is asserted as much to convince Dickens psychologically as it is to teach us. The plot is typical of almost any of Dickens's novels: money and the selfishness which makes money, ver-
sus love. As usual, one of his responses to the argument is the
fortuitous existence of a benevolent man, here doubled as the
Cheeryble brothers; "benevolence" means "charity" and "heart"
—words taken from Dickens's description of the brothers in his
preface—plus money. His other response appears at the end of
the novel, just as it does in most of the novels from this one
through *Our Mutual Friend*; it is that love is better than money.
As Mr. Charles Cheeryble tells Nicholas in bestowing Madeline

Bray's love and her small fortune on him, "you have a greater fortune in her, sir, than you would have in money were it forty times told" (NN, p. 812). Earlier, the narrator remarks of Ralph Nickleby that "Gold . . . lost its lustre in his eyes, for there were countless treasures of the heart which it could never purchase" (NN, p. 401).

The novel begins with the miser and develops, again like *Oliver Twist*, from the evils of this world to the good which is created out of it. Ralph Nickleby is introduced first, as a man who has committed himself to the idea "that riches are the only true source of happiness and power. . . . that there [is] nothing like money" (NN, p. 3). Foreshadowing John Chester in *Barnaby Rudge*, Ralph does not believe in love. When told that his brother, Nicholas's father, has "died of a broken heart," he replies, "Pooh! . . . there's no such thing. . . . a broken heart!—nonsense, it's the cant of the day. If a man can't pay his debts, he dies of a broken heart" (NN, p. 23). He later calls "all love . . . the cant of boys and girls" (NN, p. 431).

Ralph's character is that of a man of the world in the sense of being at one with it. That such evil as he represents is basic and pervasive enrages Dickens throughout the novel. "The world," he says at the outset, is "a conventional phrase which, being interpreted, often signifieth all the rascals in it" (NN, p. 28). As it is so often and in almost every novel, London is a "wilderness" (NN, p. 450). Dickens sees in Nicholas's thoughts the dark vision of evils bred by poverty and cruel neglect, and wonders at "how much injustice, misery, and wrong there was, and yet how the world rolled on, from year to year" (NN, p. 693). Madly, Ralph Nickleby characterizes the world truly—as Dickens sees it—in his last words before his suicide. He cries out in answer to the distant ringing of a bell:

> "Ring merrily for births that make expectants writhe, and for marriages that are made in hell, and toll ruefully for the dead whose shoes are worn already! Call men to prayers who are godly because not found

out, and ring chimes for the coming in of every year that brings this cursed world nearer to its end." (NN, p. 806)

What Dickens must find out is whether, if this "cursed world" is brought to an end, a blessed one can be born in its place?

I have suggested in the preface and in discussing *Oliver Twist* that Dickens has a serious imaginative attachment to Eden. In this novel he uses Eden suggestively and descriptively to clarify his visions of the world as it is and the world as it should become. The first appearance of this mythic garden is in an ironic context, in the opening description of Ralph Nickleby's house, which is similar, Dickens says, to many London houses. They often have "a melancholy little plot of ground behind them. . . . People sometimes call these dark yards 'gardens'; it is not supposed that they were ever planted, but rather that they are pieces of unreclaimed land, with the withered vegetation of the original brickfield. No man thinks of walking in this desolate place, or of turning it to any account" (NN, p. 8). This is Eden without the order that made it Paradise; this is the world of the primordial chaos —or it is the world after Eden, when everything has returned to darkness and chaos.

From his desperation with the postlapsarian world Dickens turns to look for light and order through love. On the way to Dotheboys Hall he introduces two elderly gentlemen who tell stories. They disappear during the course of the journey; they are types, however, of the benevolent man, and prepare for the later introduction of the Cheeryble brothers. Both of their stories are interesting, and, like the stories in *Pickwick Papers*, are more than just interpolated tales. The first story, of "The Five Sisters of York," is a miniature version of Dickens's developing myth of the way of the world. It begins with the five fair sisters living in seclusion in their old house "within a pleasant orchard" (NN, p. 58), from which they daily dispense charities and go to perform good works. The youngest sister is an inspiration to the rest, and of her the narrator says:

"If we all had hearts like those which beat so lightly in the bosoms of the young and beautiful, what a heaven this earth would be! If, while our bellies grow old and withered, our hearts could but retain their early youth and freshness, of what avail would be our sorrows and sufferings! But, the faint image of Eden which is stamped upon them in childhood, chafes and rubs in our rough struggles with the world, and soon wears away; too often to leave nothing but a mournful blank remaining." (NN, p. 57)

The Wordsworthian aspect of this sentiment is carried on in the tale as part of their mother's dying request that they keep at their "maidenly pursuits," weaving richly colored tapestries, or samplers. Hours passed thus, they are told, will "prove the happiest and most peaceful of our lives, and . . . if, in later times, we [go] forth into the world, and [mingle] with its cares and trials —if . . . we ever [forget] that love and duty which should bind, in holy ties, the children of one loved parent—a glance at the old work of our common pursuit [will] awaken good thoughts of by-gone days, and soften our hearts to affection and love" (NN, pp. 59-60). A monk argues against this occupation, urging that they "shun all such thoughts and chances, and, in the peaceful shelter of the church, devote your lives to Heaven" (NN, p. 60).

The younger sister answers the monk, speaking of "heaven" as "air," and of death as but the end of life. "Barter not the light and air of heaven," she says to her sisters; "Nature's own blessings are the proper goods of life, and we may share them sinlessly together. To die is our heavy portion, but, oh, let us die with life about us; when our cold hearts cease to beat, let warm hearts be beating near. . . . Dear sisters, let us live and die . . . in this green garden's compass" (NN, p. 60). She rejects a life of prayer "in peaceful shelter" from the world, to guarantee a happiness hereafter; she seems also to believe that they are living still in the first garden of Eden, "sinlessly," not in its diminished, walled-in replica. But through her speech Dickens is certainly insisting to himself that one must solve the problem of this world in this world.[2]

From this point onward in Dickens's career, the primary urge in the mythic time of this world is back toward Eden or, sometimes, to the time of the second "creation," after the Deluge. The great symbols of his fiction become the primordial beginnings of the world, Eden, the time of the Flood, and Noah's Ark; frequently associated with these in Dickens's mythology are two other symbols of the breakdown of order in civilization's history, the tower of Babel and the city of Babylon. These symbolic references come to replace, for the most part, faith in "Heaven" and the dream of escape from the world. The great vision of chaos, of the world as it is for Dickens, takes its symbolic expression as the "wilderness" of the beginning, Babel, Babylon, or the Deluge; and out of the chaos, to begin anew, come the inhabitants of Dickens's many Edens and hopeful Noah's Arks. The images of the disordered world never disappear from Dickens's fiction, nor do the symbols which represent it; but after *David Copperfield* and its tests, which prove the inadequacy of Arks and Edens as retreats, these symbols are reconstituted in Dickens's mythic vision. Weak characters continue to fabricate false Edens and hoped-for-Arks, indicating the inadequacy of the dreamy hope of innocence. Strong characters see the chaos as it is, and in terms of both myth and reality they work to change the ruined world, to

---

2. Alice, the youngest sister, dies. She goes, the narrator says, to "Heaven." The other four sisters, having experienced the world and its wounds, return to the old place, widowed. They are urged again by the monk to enter a convent, and pray. But Alice's Eden has changed, even as their lives have changed. Instead of its earlier sunny innocence and green freshness, now "the boughs of the orchard trees drooped and ran wild upon the ground," and "the grass was coarse and high"; but "it was the same orchard still," and "there was yet the spot on which they had so often sat together, when change and sorrow were but names" (NN, p. 64). Rather than forsake this place, however, and the lives and promises of life begun there, to "bow down in prayer" (NN, p. 64) in a cloister, they immortalize those early days in five stained glass replicas of their samplers in a window in the cathedral.

move it again toward Paradise. When the Flood comes, they build their own Arks, and act out Noah for themselves.

In *Nicholas Nickleby* Eden is sentimentalized badly in its association with Smike. When the poor broken boy dies—holding sacred to the last his silent love for Kate Nickleby—he sees in a vision the world Dickens longs so much to see realized. He speaks of "beautiful gardens . . . stretched out before him . . . filled with figures of men, women, and many children, all with light upon their faces." He whispers that this place is "Eden," and dies (NN, p. 763). The good people of the novel—the Cheeryble brothers, Nicholas and Kate, Frank Cheeryble, Madeline Bray, Tim Linkinwater and Miss LaCreevy, John and 'Tilda Browdie; and they are good because they love, because they have "affections" and "feelings" and sympathetic "hearts"—all strive to create the Eden Smike sees at his death. When they were at Dotheboys Hall, Smike once asked Nicholas, innocently, "is the world as bad and dismal as this place?" Nicholas responded, "Heaven forbid" (NN, p. 144). But it was not "Heaven" that kept the world from being altogether "bad and dismal" for Smike; it was Nicholas and his charity, and the good offices of those who made for him his first home. Nicholas defines "home" as "the place where, in default of a better, those I love are gathered together" (NN, p. 443). As Mr. Lillyvick says, home is "the whole framework of society," and Mr. Crummles responds that love is "the best and tenderest feelings" (NN, p. 328). For Dickens home and the love that goes with it must be strengthened and cultivated if any order is to be found in this world. Mr. Charles Cheeryble preaches a sermon on the subject to Nicholas:

> "Natural affections and instincts, my dear sir, are the most beautiful of the Almighty's works, but like other beautiful works of his, they must be reared and fostered, or it is as natural that they should be wholly obscured, and that new feelings should usurp their place, as it is that the sweetest productions of the earth, left untended, should be choked with weeds and briars." (NN, p. 596)

Ralph Nickleby's garden—like so many gardens in this distracted, forgetful world—is overgrown, literally and metaphorically, in just this disordered way; and Ralph dies, cursing both the world and his own life.[3] Ralph's last words are "Throw me on a dunghill, and let me rot there, to infect the air" (NN, p. 806). His death is like his life, and the dunghill—like the dust heaps in *Our Mutual Friend*, the image of decay, of that kind of disorder that is decomposition or disintegration—is his proper end.

Smike's end—and Smike turns out to be Ralph Nickleby's bastard son—was a vision of Eden. Following the same pattern as that of *Oliver Twist*, Dickens proves that vision in this life at the end of the novel. Nicholas and Madeline, Fred Cheeryble and Kate, and eventually Tim Linkinwater and Miss LaCreevy, are united in marriage. The brothers retire, but only after they have ordered some part of a right future by arranging these marriages. Just before the end they host a great dinner. As a party, it ignores all class distinctions—and *Nicholas Nickleby* is, among many other things, Dickens's first direct attack on the idea of a class society. The party is introduced as the most famous dinner "since the world began" (NN, p. 817). In the symbolic terms of the novel, it is just that. It is a kind of commencement dinner, marking the beginning of a new world for Dickens, conceived on the principles of love, honest affection, and true and useful morality—"heart," in a word. And in the final paragraph Dickens recurs to Smike's last dream of Eden and makes it come as true as he can upon his grave:

> The grass was green above the dead boy's grave, and trodden by feet so small and light, that not a daisy drooped its head beneath their pressure. Through all the spring and summertime, garlands of fresh

---

3. The sisters' garden in the tale becomes overgrown, too, and they resolve the problem, curiously, by immortalizing in art the order they once knew, rather than by working to reclaim their orchard's beauty.

flowers, wreathed by infant hands, rested on the stone; and, when the children came there to change them lest they should wither and be pleasant to him no longer, their eyes filled with tears, and they spoke low and softly of their poor dead cousin. (NN, p. 813)

This miraculous vision is the fulfillment of Smikes's last dream. The meaning of the scene for Dickens has its roots in the narrative remark, early in the novel, that "things that are changed or gone will come back as they used to be, thank God! in sleep" (NN, p. 42).[4]

At this stage, Dickens is still too disturbed by the enormity of the chaos in the real world to abandon the retreat of dreams. Yet there is more of a commitment to realistic endeavor and its realistic effect here than there was in *Oliver Twist*—more, too, than there is in *The Old Curiosity Shop*, the novel which follows *Nicholas Nickleby*. *The Old Curiosity Shop*, like *Oliver Twist*, is premised on the sentiments of Christian faith; and in both instances this faith undermines the structure of the novel. In each instance the central character is idealized as a character, and is kept an innocent child. Master Humphrey, the narrator of *The Old Curiosity Shop*, "grieves . . . to contemplate the initiation of children into the ways of life" (OCS, p. 6)—and Nell is thus kept out of it. But Nicholas is a young man, growing up into the real world. He is the ancestor of a dozen Dickensian young men, each of whom in the process of growing up strives to comprehend the world, and for the sake of whose maturity Dickens abandons dreams and sentimental visions and engages himself earnestly with reality.

There is very little of the undercoating of orthodox piety in *Nicholas Nickleby*. At Nicholas's father's death he vainly com-

---

4. Cf. "Dreams are the bright creatures of poem and legend, who sport on earth in the night season, and melt away in the first beam of the sun, which lights grim care and stern reality in their daily pilgrimage through the world" (NN, p. 146). See also the sentiments of Master Humphrey from *Master Humphrey's Clock*, quoted below, p. 32.

mends his wife and children, "to One who never deserted the widow or her fatherless children" (NN, p. 5). Otherwise, the references to religion and Christian morality are all ironic or satiric, as they were in *Pickwick Papers*. Mr. Brooker speaks Dickens's indictment against organized religion: that "the Lord's Prayer . . . as it is offered up in cities like this, is understood to include half the luxuries of the world for the rich, and just as much coarse food as will support life for the poor" (NN, p. 572). The chief spokesman for "morality" and "Providence" is Wackford Squeers, the cruel headmaster at Dotheboys Hall. He insists he exerts a "moral influence" over the boys, by mistreating them physically and mentally (NN, p. 782), and he declares himself to be "guaranteed, by unimpeachable references, to be a out-and-outer in morals and uprightness of principle" (NN, p. 780). He refers to his code of instructing children as "going according to the scripter" (NN, p. 740), and advises his greedy son always to "do them things that you see your father do, and when you die you'll go right slap to Heaven" (NN, p. 497). Dickens denies himself the fantasy of thinking this world an Eden in *Nicholas Nickleby*, and by letting Squeers appropriate heaven he frees himself from the temptation to indulge in pieties of heaven as an alternative to this chaotic place. And thus, though the novel is probably Dickens's least successful as a work of fiction, it is important for his development as a novelist. He looks at this world in *Nicholas Nickleby*, and at "all the rascals in it"; and for the first time he refuses to be distracted by what he sees.

4

The Old Curiosity Shop is filled with talk of going to heaven; and it is told by Master Humphrey—the identification is an afterthought, surely—who is fond of such things as an "air-built castle" (OCS, p. 1) and who would prefer, as he says in *Master Humphrey's Clock*, "to ramble through the world in a pleasant dream, rather than ever waken again to its harsh realities"

(MHC, p. 11). The combination of the dreamer and his dream with Dickens's fear of the evil of the real world accounts for the novel's morbidity and sentimentality. The dream is of death and heaven as it was in *Oliver Twist*. It takes Nell and her grandfather out of the life of the novel, in effect, leaving them abstracted wanderers on the road to never-never land. Their absence from the real world of *The Old Curiosity Shop*, which occurs as early as chapter six, leaves the stage clear for the vital battle between good and evil, order and chaos. Daniel Quilp embodies the evidence of evil and chaos, Mr. Garland the force of goodness and order. Nell is on neither side. Indeed, through the intrusion of Nell and this morbid dream of heaven, Dickens almost makes the tension of the novel a contest between life and death; and both the good and the evil are on the side of life.

London is the primary place of the novel, again, the place from which Nell and her grandfather flee, usually to churchyards, where, like Oliver, Nell finds "a curious kind of pleasure in lingering among [the] houses of the dead" (OCS, p. 128). The city's general aspect is that of a "labyrinth" (OCS, p. 114), full of "rotting houses, many to let, many yet building, many half-built and mouldering away" (OCS, p. 115)—which image must be the most typically Dickensian image, appearing in a form similar to this in every novel from *Oliver Twist* through *Our Mutual Friend*; in every novel, that is, after *Pickwick Papers*. The city is "heaped in rank confusion," a "Babel" (OCS, pp. 115-16) of "brick-fields, skirting gardens paled with staves of old casks, or timber pillaged from houses burnt down and blackened and blistered by the flames—rounds of dockweed, nettles, coarse grass and oyster-shells" (OCS, p. 115). The "blighted" industrial city, Birmingham, which Nell and her grandfather pass through on their way to the West, also participates in this archetypal disorder: "Dismantled houses here and there appeared, tottering to the earth, propped up by fragments of others that had fallen down, unroofed, windowless, blackened, desolate, but yet inhabited," in the midst of the hellish, "interminable perspective of brick towers, never ceasing in their black vomit, blasting all things living or inanimate" (OCS, pp. 335-36).

All of this chaos is condensed, in terms of human evil, into Quilp. Mrs. Nubbles "really don't believe he's human" (OCS, p. 362), he is so grotesque. His favorite haunt is what he calls "a little summer-house overlooking the river," which the narrator describes as "a rugged wooden box, rotten and bare to see, which overhung the river's mud, and threatened to slide down into it" (OCS, pp. 161-62).

> The tavern to which it belonged was a crazy building, sapped and undermined by the rats, and only upheld by great bars of wood which were reared against its walls, and had propped it up so long that even they were decaying and yielding with their load. . . . The house stood —if anything so old and feeble could be said to stand—on a piece of waste ground, blighted with the unwholesome smoke of factory chimneys. (OCS, p. 162)

The "appropriate name" for this "choice retreat" of Quilp's, we are told, is "the Wilderness" (OCS, pp. 171, 381, 382, 384, 414). Opposed to Quilp's chaos are the person of Mr. Garland and the world he inhabits. Along with the single gentleman (Master Humphrey) Mr. Garland is another example of the benevolent man. He and Mrs. Garland live in "a beautiful little cottage" (OCS, p. 168), "with everything in it . . . bright and glowing, and . . . precisely ordered" (OCS, p. 170). There is a room "just the size for Kit," and "a little stable, just the size for the pony." There is a "garden . . . bright with flowers in full bloom," of "charming and elegant appearance," where "there was not a weed to be seen," thanks to the daily labors of Mr. Garland. "Everything, within the house and without, seemed to be the perfection of neatness and order" (OCS, p. 168). It is to this world—and to the idea of order that it represents—that Mr. Garland attracts the good people of the novel, defeating Quilp, and his agents, the legal Brasses, in contest for Kit and Dick Swiveller.

It is conceivable that, had not Nell and her grandfather existed, Dick Swiveller would have been the hero of *The Old Curiosity Shop*. He is an early brother of Sidney Carton and Eugene Wrayburn, certainly, in both character and circumstance, and has all the qualities of life necessary for a Dickensian hero. Dick is caught between the two positive forces, of good and evil, order and chaos; and through the agency of Fred Trent, Nell's brother, he is involved in the negative force of dream and death as well. In the end we are much better satisfied seeing Richard "creating" the Marchioness, and marrying her, than we would have been seeing him marry Nell. And the same holds true for Kit; his early affection for Nell was disturbing. His marriage with Barbara is a happy one, and produces four children, though he still keeps Nell's memory alive, and teaches his children "how she had gone to Heaven, as all good people did" (OCS, p. 554).

The sentimentalism of Nell's part in the novel begins with the narrator, Master Humphrey. It is his story, and he is "always grieve[d] . . . to contemplate the initiation of children into the ways of life, when they are scarcely more than infants" (OCS, p. 6). It is Master Humphrey who first thinks of Nell as a "fairy" (OCS, p. 5), and he is the one who describes Nell's quiet afternoon high up in the church tower, looking out at "everything, so beautiful and happy," as "like passing from death to life; it was drawing her nearer Heaven" (OCS, p. 398). He believes, insistently, in "another world, where sin and sorrow never came; a tranquil place of rest, where nothing evil entered" (OCS, p. 401). These sentiments are infectious in Dickens. Mrs. Nubbles has visions of a secular never-never land where Nell and her grandfather have gone with all the money, and "where it can't be taken away from them, and they will never be disturbed" (OCS, p. 153). The schoolmaster has been taught by his griefs in the world to hold a holier, more mystical faith than Mrs. Nubbles's, and he insists at Nell's death that she has gone to "Heaven's justice," from which no one could wish to "call her back to life" (OCS, p. 539).

Living alongside this faith in heaven is another faith, which is vital rather than morbid; a faith in the efficacy of simple goodness. The schoolmaster proposes it first: "There is nothing . . . no, nothing innocent or good, that dies, and is forgotten. Let us hold to that faith, or none" (OCS, p. 406). This sentiment is repeated in the end of the novel, as the single gentleman, the schoolmaster, and the bachelor bury Nell. They experience a Wordsworthian vision, as "all outward things and inward thoughts teem with assurances of immortality." What follows, however, is not an apostrophe to heaven, but Dickens's assertion of faith in the continuing influence of goodness, through suffering:

> When Death strikes down the innocent and young, for every form from which he lets the panting spirit free, a hundred virtues rise, in shapes of mercy, charity, and love, to walk the world, and bless it. Of every tear that sorrowing mortals shed on such green graves, some good is born, some gentler nature comes. (OCS, p. 544)

The proof of this belief that goodness will "walk the world" comes not in escape and retreat now, but in what Dickens sees as a contribution to the real progress of the world. In this *The Old Curiosity Shop* is an advance for Dickens from *Oliver Twist*. Nell, with her grandfather, has lived in retreat from the world, and dies, retreating into heaven. But the good people who have known her, or who have been interested in her, end the novel committed to this world and to the propagation of goodness in it. The bachelor eventually comes to live with the Garlands. The single gentleman goes "forth into the world, a lover of his kind" (OCS, p. 553), his rich benevolence limited only by his continuing bachelorhood. Dick Swiveller, "recovering very slowly from his illness" (OCS, p. 551)—but recovering a changed man[5]—

---

5. Pip and Eugene Wrayburn are changed by their illnesses, too. An excel-

undertakes the education and development of the Marchioness. They are married, and, we are told, "played many hundred thousand games of cribbage together" (OCS, p. 552); strangely, for Dickens, they do not have any children.[6] But Kit—"of course he married" (OCS, p. 554)—and Barbara have four children, at latest count. And a wife is found for Abel Garland: "How it happened . . . nobody knows. But certain it is that in course of time they were married; and equally certain it is that they were the happiest of the happy" (OCS, p. 550).

As Dickens creates this future for Abel, Adam's good son, he identifies again his idea for the reclamation of this disordered world: "And it is pleasant to write down that they reared a family; because any propagation of goodness and benevolence is no small addition to the aristocracy of nature, and no small subject of rejoicing for mankind at large" (OCS, p. 550).

The idea of "the propagation of goodness and benevolence" is akin to Dickens's faith in the influence of goodness, through suffering. Together, they form the basis for Dickens's imaginative plan for dealing with the world. Rarely after this novel will he allow anyone to retreat from the world into the safety of a little pocket of love. Good people will go "forth into the world," more or less certainly, to work for its change and betterment. Rarely after this will Dickens let himself be distracted from this chaotic world of "harsh realities" by "pleasant dreams" of heaven, or never-never land. His talents are needed, not in "another world, where sin and sorrow never came; a tranquil place of rest, where nothing evil entered" (OCS, p. 401), but in this world.

---

lent dissertation has been written on the whole subject, by Robert J. Heaman: "Love and Adversity in the Novels of Charles Dickens" (Ph.D. diss., The University of Michigan, 1969).

6. Dale Simmerman has pointed out to me that "cribbage" contains a pun on where you keep babies—in cribs; so perhaps "many hundred thousand games of cribbage" is a better substitute for children for Swiveller and the Marchioness than it might at first seem.

2

BARNABY RUDGE, MARTIN CHUZZLEWIT, AND DOMBEY AND SON

1

To say that *Barnaby Rudge* is dickens's challenge to Walter Scott—on Scott's own grounds—is a half-truth that is rather misleading. *Barnaby Rudge* is not a romance, but a Dickens novel; and as such it has a substance that not even Scott's *Heart of Midlothian* had. It is that substance, rather than simply the excitement and interest of the novel, that I wish to discuss.

Barnaby Rudge is a number of novels. It is in part an historical novel; but it uses its historical setting to criticize religion as a fractious force in society, and religious piety as cant, hypocrisy, and cruel sham. It also contains Dickens's first serious and elaborated attack on idleness and the evils of a class society, though this attack has nothing directly to do with the historical situation. Most significantly, it is a novel in every way concerned with violence and excess, a novel full of Dickens's sense of the need for change, and his imaginative interest in the various revolutionary forces that would overthrow the established order of society. Dickens despises privilege and prejudice, but he also fears anarchy. In the end one feels a bit uneasy. A great deal of the world of the novel has been destroyed, by fire; but yet one knows that not enough of the evil has been burned out, and Dickens knows this, too, that men always stop any revolution short of its self-destructive climax. Still, the typical symbolic regeneration of the world—marriages, and children—takes place at the end of the novel.

Dickens usually associates human characteristics with natural description, so that the world described exists in metaphorical relation to a certain character or characters. Or, to put it the other way around—and this, I think, is the proper sequence—Dickens envisions the world, and then creates characters who exist in symbolic identification with that world. Thus Daniel Quilp is linked with the "Wilderness" in *Nicholas Nickleby*, and the Garlands with order. In *Barnaby Rudge*, all evil—at least, all the different kinds of evil—condense into the man of society, John Chester. It is Chester who speaks for the "natural class distinctions" (BR, p. 200) in society, and who is himself the personification of privileged indolence. He is also the conscious perverter of the idea of morality, and the character who denies the existence of love. Some of Dickens's best energy is exerted in his creation—as is usual with the exhibition of evil in Dickens's world. Chester's relations in Dickens's imagination are such various characters as Ralph Nickleby, Harold Skimpole in *Bleak House*, and Alfred Lammle in *Our Mutual Friend*. As a gentleman he is also in some way Pip's ancestor; and indirectly it is Chester who is "blown up" in the end of *Our Mutual Friend*, when Twemlow challenges the "Voice of Society."

Chester's "graceful indolence" (BR, p. 95), his "complacency, indolence, and satisfaction" (BR, p. 113), his life of "luxury and idleness" are so infuriatingly real, and, symbolically, so lifeless.[1]

---

1. He speaks a brilliant paragraph to his son that could epitomize the conversation of any of several of Oscar Wilde's characters: "I observe another fly in

He is "liberally educated," and thus is "fit for nothing" (BR, p. 116). Working from his own self-knowledge, and drawing the analogy therefrom, he is sure "that our globe itself is hollow," or "should be, if Nature is consistent in her works" (BR, p. 91). Chester treats the world as he values himself—hypocritically, and cynically. His best teacher is Chesterfield, in whose every page he finds "some captivating hypocrisy" (BR, p. 174). He finds in this master "the finest code of morality . . . in the universe" (BR, p. 173) and from this, one supposes, becomes himself so concerned with "morality." He warns his son Ned—in arguing that he must marry a fortune, and not "a Catholic, unless she was amazingly rich"—that we must "be moral, Ned, or we are nothing" (BR, p. 121). For Chester, "fine feelings," "affections," "moral and religious feeling," all must have money as their highest aim and reward (BR, p. 94). When young Ned refuses to conduct himself according to these precepts, he is dismissed by his father: "Go, sir, since you have no moral sense remaining" (BR, p. 246).

In his cunning attack upon the pious Mrs. Varden, Chester plays the word "morality" as his trump card, and wins:

". . . if we are not sincere, we are nothing. Nothing upon earth. Let us be sincere, my dear madam—"

"—and Protestant," murmured Mrs. Varden.

"—and Protestant above all things. Let us be sincere and Protestant, strictly moral, strictly just (though always with a leaning towards mercy), strictly honest, and strictly true, and . . . we throw up a groundwork and foundation, so to speak, of goodness, on which we may afterwards erect some worthy superstructure." (BR, p. 206)

Mrs. Varden is seduced by this cant, and thinks him "a perfect character . . . a meek, righteous, thoroughgoing Christian." The

---

the cream-jug, but have the goodness not to take it out as you did the first, for their walk when their legs are milky is extremely ungraceful and disagreeable" (BR, p. 119).

"superstructure" this "Christian" would make, however, is the hollow one which such "accomplished gentlemen . . . in society" (BR, p. 183) as himself call the "moral" world.

Chester's cynical hypocrisy—his favorite form of farewell is "God bless you" (BR, pp. 121, 202), which "fervent blessing" he finds "as easy as cursing . . . and more becoming to the face" (BR, p. 202)—makes him deny the existence of those virtues and human institutions which, for Dickens, give substance to life. "Marriage," Chester says, "is a civil contract; people marry to better their worldly condition and improve appearances; it is an affair of house and furniture, of liveries, servants, equipage, and so forth" (BR, p. 244). Like Ralph Nickleby, he refuses to allow any figurative sense of the word "heart," insisting that "the heart is an ingenious part of our formation . . . which has no more to do with what you say or think than your knees have" (BR, p. 243). He does not believe in love: "There's no such thing" (BR, p. 116). Dickens's novel, of course, disproves Chester's contention, and the sham order of manners is replaced by the true ordering principle of love. Chester is destroyed; Dolly Varden is changed and saved, marries Joe Willet, and raises a large family; Ned Chester marries Emma Haredale, and they produce "a family almost as numerous as Dolly's" (BR, p. 634).

This is the story that is played out in the natural world of *Barnaby Rudge*, to which the historical situation may seem but incidental. Three other characters—Gabriel Varden, his wife, and Barnaby Rudge, a "natural" boy—are important to the story, however, and they are its links with the Gordon riots. Gabriel Varden is the good man who insists on doing his work as a locksmith and a human being; his wife carries as her blunt sword of cant and prejudice the "Protestant Manual," with which she torments Gabriel and everyone else. Gabriel is "a chirping, healthy, honest-hearted fellow, who made the best of everything, and felt kindly towards everybody," who, even "if he had sat in a jolting waggon, full of rods of iron . . . would have brought some harmony out of it" (BR, p. 307). He is the stabilizing good figure, who sets the example of simple honor, integrity, and love for the novel: "A better creature never lived" (BR, p. 605). Finally, he is the savior of poor Barnaby.

The larger natural world of *Barnaby Rudge*, the world in which this drama is played, is that of the Gordon riots of 1780. There are three aspects of this period of crisis which concern Dickens, and thus become a part of the novel. First, as religious disturbances, the Gordon riots represent for him the madness of religious sectarianism and the irrelevance of religious doctrines. Second, the riots are connected with a social revolution which calls for "another state of society" (BR, p. 203), "an altered state of society" (BR, pp. 300, 392). Dickens puts the revolutionary side of the riots in the hands of Sim Tappertit, and then refuses to take it seriously. He seems actually to fear this movement as he creates it, whereas he only despises religious factionalism, and pities "the deluded lord" (BR, p. 271), George Gordon. The third aspect of the riots, for Dickens, is symbolic. As a symbolic phenomenon, the riots come as the curse of madness and fire upon a city needing to be razed. London is, as usual, that "great city, which lay . . . like a dark shadow on the ground, reddening the sluggish air with a deep, dull light." It is made up of "labyrinths of public ways and shops, and swarms of busy people. . . . tall steeples looming in the air, and piles of unequal roofs oppressed by chimneys." It is "visible in the darkness by its own faint light, and not by the light of heaven" (BR, p. 26). This "heaven" means both Heaven and the stars, surely; thus London's phosphorescent glow is the sign of its corruption. In a candid moment with his son, Chester characterizes London—or the civilization it represents—as a world in which "the law, the church, the court, the camp . . . the stock exchange, the pulpit, the counting-house, the royal drawing room, the senate" are all distracted and corrupt (BR, p. 119). This is the world that is set to the torch.

The relationship between the riots and the Chester-Haredale-

Willet-Varden part of the novel is also symbolic. The riots extend from London to the Maypole Inn, and destroy it. Old John Willet, who has always complained about his son's lack of "imagination," having not the imagination himself to believe in the riots even happening, is so shocked by the rioters' arrival at the Maypole that he never recovers from it. The rioters go on, then, to destroy the Haredale house, called the Warren. What is burned out at the Warren is an old, unsolved family murder, and the prejudice which has perverted the character of Mr. Haredale and kept Emma in seclusion. Mr. Haredale kills John Chester on the grounds of the ruined house, and then flees to a religious and penitential "refuge from the world" (BR, p. 628). Ned and Emma do not rebuild the Warren, but choose instead to live in London—, in the real world, to work, symbolically, in its rebuilding. Joe Willet (who served honorably as a soldier during the riots) and Dolly reopen the Maypole, and add to it a farm and Barnaby. Barnaby, we are told, "recovered by degrees" from his ordeal, and "became, in other respects, more rational." He is happy on the Maypole farm, as "husbandman," but "never could be tempted into London" (BR, pp. 633-34).

Thus the worlds of the novel are woven together. The London of the riots of 1780 is symbolically (and psychologically, for Dickens) civilization at a time of crisis. The crisis came once before, in our mythology, in the form of a flood. We are warned that the next time it comes it should be by fire, and it is this myth, rather than that of the Deluge, that Dickens uses in *Barnaby Rudge*. The revolution of *A Tale of Two Cities* is called "the deluge of the year One of Liberty" (TTC, p. 259); but here revolution brings fire, historically, and Dickens uses that fire for the great one prophesied for our last crisis. Yet the world doesn't end in *Barnaby Rudge*; it did not end in England with the Gordon riots. After the crisis is passed, there is a time for rebuilding, for the serious work of trying to remake and reorder the world—properly, this time. It takes strong men for the job;

not all men can do it. Ned and Emma work in the world, and raise a family: the first is a sign of this dedication, and the second a mythical promise of their work's success. Although Gabriel Varden's shop, "the Golden Key," is invaded by the rioters, he reopens it—"with a new coat of paint upon the sign" showing "more bravely even than in days of yore" (BR, p. 604)—almost before the riots are finally over. Joe and Dolly render good and generous services at the Maypole, Dolly having been won by Joe from her youthful coquettishness "to know myself" and "to be something better than I was" (BR, p. 602). And they are "happy in this world—which is not an utterly miserable one, with all its faults" (BR, p. 602).

Barnaby's fear of London concludes the novel. It is impossible to know if Dickens's fear of chaos is still with him in Barnaby's terror and "repugnance," and the future described for Ned and Emma only his hope and dream; or if his commitment to the work of order in the world is represented in the careers of Ned and Emma and Mr. Varden, and Barnaby's fear and the Willets' retreat but indicative, then, of lesser occupations and obligations in the mythical society of the earthly good.

2

This mythic conception of life and the world surfaces metaphorically in the rich ironies of *Martin Chuzzlewit*. Dickens thought he had written an attack on "the commonest of all the vices . . . Selfishness" (MC, p. 39). So many of the English, American, and continental novelists of the nineteenth century wrote, or thought they wrote, to some such "object" (MC, p. 39). If we read *Martin Chuzzlewit* as such a purposeful "exhibition" (MC, p. 42) it is quickly a dull, crude, and imaginatively pointless moral story. But if we look at it in the larger context of Dickens's mythic conception, the experience of the novel is significant. *Martin Chuzzlewit* is the first of Dickens's novels to make precisely clear the significance and relevance of this myth. Here

41

"Eden" exists not only as the organizing myth of Dickens's vision, but also in an actual, metaphorical identity, in "the New World," in America. "Eden"—the "settlement" that is "a grave" (MC, p. 516)—exists satirically in Dickens's caricature of America, but it exists as a real place in Martin's and Mark Tapley's adventures there; and it also exists in a complex ironic way in relation to England and to the dreams and ambitions of Martin and Mark.

The first of these identities is unimportant; for all of the heavy-handed satire, Dickens only proves the relationship of the new world to the old. On both sides of the ocean of Martin's and Mark's travels there is hypocrisy and greed; on both sides men sham class, and base everything, including their own identities, on money. Mr. Hannibal Chollop (MC, p. 522), Mr. Jefferson Brick (MC, p. 272), General Fladdock (MC, p. 289), Mr. Norris (MC, p. 291), and General Choke (MC, pp. 347, 399) are all fond of the word "moral" in their speech—which proves only that Mr. Pecksniff does not have a monopoly on the canting abuse of that term. Dickens inveighs with broad descriptive indignation against the coarse brutality of American manners—and condemns Pecksniffian hypocrisy just as well. Martin complains, for Dickens, against a society whose "Institutions" are—and still are!—"pistols with revolving barrels, swordsticks, bowie-knives ... shooting down and stabbing in the streets" (MC, p. 535); and back in England, young Jonas Chuzzlewit plots a patricide, bludgeons Montague Tigg to death, and poisons himself. "Dishonour and Fraud are among the Institutions of the great republic" of the new world, an example being the misrepresented Eden; and paralleling this fraud in England is Tigg's Anglo-Bengalee Disinterested Loan and Life Assurance Company.

The dramatic reality of Eden, as it is described, is also linked with Dickens's England. Eden is not unique, or uniquely American; it is the familiar epitome of chaos which Dickens sees and images in every novel after *Pickwick Papers*. The "Eden Settlement" (MC, p. 353) is advertised as a "thriving city" (MC, p. 357), an "earthly Paradise" (MC, p. 363) from which "nobody as goes . . . ever comes back a-live" (MC, p. 373). In conception, Eden is "An Architectural city! There were banks, churches, cathedrals, market-places, factories, hotels, stores, mansions, wharves; an exchange, a theatre; public buildings of all kinds" (MC, p. 355). Actually, it is

A flat morass, bestrewn with fallen timber; a marsh on which the good growth of the earth seemed to have been wrecked and cast away, that from its decomposing ashes vile and ugly things might rise; where the very trees took the aspect of huge weeds, begotten of the slime from which they sprung, by the hot sun that burnt them up. (MC, p. 377)[2]

Taking "a rough survey of the settlement," Mark sees

not above a score of cabins in the whole; half of these appeared un-tenanted; all were rotten and decayed. The most tottering, abject, and forlorn among them was called, with great propriety, the Bank, and National Credit Office. It had some feeble props about it, but was settling deep down in the mud, past all recovery.

Here and there an effort had been made to clear the land, and something like a field had been marked out, where, among the stumps and ashes of burnt trees, a scanty crop of Indian corn was growing. In some quarters, a snake or zig-zag fence had been begun, but in no instance had it been completed; and the fallen logs, half hidden in the soil, lay mouldering away. . . . A fetid vapour, hot and sickening as

---

2. An analysis of Dickens's style here proves an interesting point. The description of Eden as it actually exists is formally structured rhetoric, both syntactically and rhythmically. The fantasy description of Eden, however, is an orderless, logicless catalog, a jumble of things, of "buildings." I would suggest that the formless description represents in its formlessness the failure—the necessary failure—of the Eden experiment, and that it even represents the necessary failure of our civilization so long as we base our civilization on collections of buildings. It could be demonstrated that more and more through the course of his career Dickens uses catalogs of seemingly randomly collected items and crazy repetitions to describe and define chaos, and that these catalogs are the linguistic base from which he makes his fictions.

the breath of an oven, rose up from the earth, and hung on everything around. . . .

Their own land was mere forest. The trees [were] tangled all together in a heap; a jungle deep and dark, with neither earth nor water at its roots, but putrid matter, formed of the pulpy offal of the two, and of their own corruption. (MC, pp. 380-81)

In the "New World," "man is in a more primeval state," and can thus be seen, according to the advertisements for Eden, "in all his dignity" (MC, p. 349). Eden is one of "the wilder gardens" (MC, p. 520), from which one sees "the stagnant morning mist, and red sun . . . the vapour rising up from land and river" (MC, p. 530). It is in so much the "primeval state" that there is "no end to the water" (MC, p. 282).

This last allusion is not just primeval; it also refers to the Flood. The ocean which Martin and Mark cross to the "New World" is called a "waste of waters" (MC, p. 245), "an eternity of troubled water" (MC, p. 246), and the ship itself is an "unwholesome ark" (MC, p. 248)[3] loaded down with "English people, Irish people, Welsh people, and Scottish people" (MC, p. 248) —which sounds like a careful representation of a sort of British "world." As Martin and Mark come into New York harbor, the ship is called an "antediluvian monster" (MC, p. 254). Eden itself first appears as if "the waters of the Deluge might have left it but a week before; so choked with slime and matted growth was the hideous swamp which bore that name" (MC, p. 377). Although this description is what makes Eden real in the novel, it also makes it real in mythic commonality with what Dickens is always seeing the world as: a place of mud and mist, of waters rising and receding, of rotting vegetation in crazy gardens, or houses toppling down and returning to the mud whence they came. This is the universal descriptive metaphor, for Dickens: the myth of the failure of order in our world.

***

3. The National Hotel, where the Watertoast Sympathizers meet, is also called an "Ark" (MC, p. 358).

The ironic identity of Eden is already partly represented in this description of the real, geographical place. But the irony of Eden is more than one of the simple misnomers applied to "that regenerated land" (MC, p. 264). As Mark knows, any real Eden should be full with "lots of serpents" (MC, p. 342). And thanks to "the curse pronounced on Adam" (MC, p. 310) one cannot expect a "terrestrial Paradise," either in Todgers's by the Monument in the City of London or in Eden itself (MC, p. 513). The world is all the same—and it is not ideal. The Chuzzlewit family, like the rest of us, are all "descended in a direct line from Adam and Eve" (MC, p. 1), "the descendants of Adam" (MC, p. 6); and in reference to the Chuzzlewits, Dickens reminds us that "there was, in that oldest family of which we have any record, a murderer and a vagabond" (MC, p. 1). There are two more references to "Cain" in the novel (MC, pp. 419, 720), and another mention of "Adam" (MC, p. 607)—as though the point of postlapsarian chaos were not already strongly enough impressed upon us.

The truth of the mythic setting comes out in the stormy night of Jonas's and Tigg's trip down into Wiltshire. Jonas plots the murder; and "the thunder rolled, the lightning flashed; the rain poured down like Heaven's wrath" (MC, p. 695). The irony is one of recognition. The point of Dickens's vision now is not just that the world is a "wilderness"—viewed from Todgers's (MC, p. 130) or from Eden (MC, p. 523)—but that one must quit building "castles in the air" (MC, p. 352) and build instead with the real bricks made from the clay of this real world. Indulgence in such airy dreams is self-indulgence, and "very selfishness" (MC, p. 352). The illusion of an ideal Eden is the same unmanly dream as the dream of escape, to which so many of Dickens's earlier characters have succumbed. A strong man—a good "man of the world" (that phrase is one of Dickens's favorites in this novel)—must lose his illusions about Eden, so that he can start to work in the real world.

Martin enters upon the American venture determined to make his fortune. "I am going to America," he tells Mary, "with great prospects of doing well" (MC, pp. 237-38), and with plans to "come gaily back, with a road through life hewn out before me" (MC, p. 241). His plan for success in the New World is the noble one of civilization: "ornamental architecture applied to domestic purposes, can hardly fail to be in great request in that country," he assumes (MC, p. 230). But as he begins to see America—as he "enlarges his circle of acquaintance; increases his stock of wisdom; and [multiplies] his own experiences" (MC, p. 278) —he begins to sense the inappropriateness of the "domestic architecture project" (MC, pp. 279-80).[4] It is not "ornamental" art which the world—or the Eden Settlement in it—needs, but the "useful" art (MC, p. 527) which will order the elements of chaos.

Like the world at large, the "architectural city" of Eden has not a single architect (MC, p. 355). When Martin and Mark arrive there, however, Martin is so depressed by what he sees—"the firmness of his nature conquered by the razing of an air-built castle" (MC, p. 379)—that he cannot set to work. Mark, however, puts out their sign, "Chuzzlewit and Co., Architects and Surveyors," sets out the tools of their trade, and remarks to Martin: "We can build the oven in the afternoon. There never was such a handy spot for clay as Eden is" (MC, p. 382).The function of the architect (and he is a prototype of the artist for Dickens) is to make and order the world, not just to "decorate" it. The raw material for this work is "handy" in Eden, in its rawest state.[5]

Three things happen to Martin in Eden. He is ill, and then when Mark falls ill he tends him in his fever. He is disillusioned

---

4. One of Pecksniff's early proposals to Martin is that he draw up plans for an "ornamental turnpike," on the assumption that such work "has a remarkable effect upon the imagination" (MC, p. 87).
5. And to make something from clay in Eden is, mythically, a highly significant act!

by Eden, and thus is disillusioned in his prospects and anticipations of success. And he changes, through these trials and the "reflection" they encourage, to become a new and stronger young man, full of "knowledge of himself" (MC, p. 525). He learns, in Eden, "with Hope so far removed, Ambition quenched, and Death beside him . . . the failing of his life," and can identify this failing: "selfishness was in his breast, and must be rooted out. . . . So low had Eden brought him down. So high had Eden raised him up" (MC, p. 525). After this crisis Mark recovers, and he and Martin prepare to return to England. While waiting to depart they "devoted such strength as they had to the attempted improvement of their land; to clearing some of it, and preparing it for useful purposes" (MC, p. 527).

Dickens brings Martin and Mark back from Eden as though bringing them back from some sort of allegorical journey. The boat they went to Eden on, indeed, seemed like "old Charon's boat" (MC, p. 375) as it carried them down the river to that hellishly ironic paradise. They return wiser, but not sadder for this experience. What Dickens has done is submit them to the direct experience of his mythic world, the world which we have known as readers in other novels through its allusive and metaphoric suggestions.

That this real but also mythic Eden in America is the same world Martin had thought to leave behind in England is clear enough, surely. Dickens refers to the relation of the two parts of the novel as that of "a dream within a dream" (MC, p. 297) to justify his first change of the scene from America back to England. Later, with Martin lying ill in Eden, he changes the scene to Pecksniff's house and has that false architect greet old Martin Chuzzlewit pretending to be "gardening" in his own Eden:

> "You find me in my garden-dress. You will excuse it, I know. It is an ancient pursuit, gardening. Primitive, my dear sir; for, if I am not mistaken, Adam was the first of our calling. My Eve, I grieve to say, is no more, sir; but . . . I do a little bit of Adam still." (MC, p. 384)

At the beginning of chapter 33, which leaves Charity Pecksniff engaging herself to Augustus Moddle for more "proceedings in Eden, and a proceeding out of it" (MC, p. 513), Dickens writes:

> From Mr. Moddle to Eden is an easy and natural transition. Mr. Moddle, living in the atmosphere of Miss Pecksniff's love, dwelt (if he had but known it) in a terrestrial Paradise. The thriving city of Eden was also a terrestrial Paradise. (MC, p. 513)

The American adventures are not a digression in *Martin Chuzzlewit*; they are essential to it—though they needn't have been to America. Elsewhere, in both *David Copperfield* and *Great Expectations*, Dickens uses Australia—distractingly—as a sort of never-never land, and he seems to take somewhat seriously its magical possibilities as "a terrestrial Paradise."[6] The American Eden in *Martin Chuzzlewit* teaches the lesson against dreams, and for hard work in the real world. This lesson does not argue against the imagination, but rather insists that the imagination be employed in the creation of a new order for this world. The tension between Martin and Mark as they set off together is not just in Martin's selfishness and Mark's selflessness, but also in Martin's dream of escaping the harsh world which has left him "disinherited" (MC, p. 93)[7] and Mark's ambition to meet the world at its worst, so that he can "come out strong" and be "jolly." One of Mark's most "hopeful wisions is, that there's a deal of misery a-waitin' for me; in the midst of which I may come out tolerable strong" (MC, p. 737). In this role, Mark is an idealized and philosophically conceived variation on Sam Weller; he is

---

6. Bernard Shaw, a good Dickensian himself, refers ironically to Australia as "a term signifying paradise, or an eternity of bliss" in his 1921 version of the Pentateuch, *Back to Methuselah*, part 4, act 2.

7. Martin tells Tom, "I have been bred up from childhood with great expectations, and have been taught to believe that I should be, one day, very rich" (MC, p. 93). One of the gentlemen whom Tigg introduces to Jonas is named "Pip," too—and "Pip's our mutual friend" (MC, p. 451).

also more the artist than Martin, though he insists humbly on being but "Co." in the firm of "Chuzzlewit and Co." Martin hopes—selfishly—to decorate the world, as a gentleman architect; Mark wants—selflessly—to build the world, to rebuild the world, even from scratch.

The end of *Martin Chuzzlewit* is one of the worst in Dickens. He has left himself so much to do—unravel the murder mystery, retrieve old Martin Chuzzlewit, give justice to Pecksniff, dispose of his daughters, marry John Westlock and Ruth, Martin and Mary, Mark and Mrs. Lupin, and settle Tom Pinch. Under the influence perhaps of so much tying up, he brings Mark's friends back from Eden, recovering them in this "Old World," as Martin had hoped, rather than "in the next one," as Mark had feared (MC, p. 529); and he resurrects Bailey junior to an irrelevant life. The crisis which brings on this conclusion is the revolution in character that marks both Martin and Tom Pinch significantly. Martin achieves a "knowledge of himself" (MC, p. 525), and is able to give up his dreams of gentlemanly success and "great expectations" (MC, p. 93). Tom achieves a better knowledge of the world, and discovers Pecksniff's "real nature" (MC, p. 482).[8]

But it is Mary who speaks of Pecksniff's "real nature"; what her disclosure discovers to Tom is something slightly different, and much more interesting. Tom discovers that Pecksniff doesn't exist—that his falseness and hypocrisy have been so complete that his entire being is a sham: first, "It was not that Pecksniff,

---

8. There is a strange connection between Pecksniff and Mr. Pickwick. Like his good predecessor's, "Mr. Pecksniff's manner was so bland, and he nodded his head so soothingly, and showed in everything such an affable sense of his own excellence, that anybody would have been comforted . . . by the mere voice and presence of such a man" (MC, pp. 32-33). Later, Pecksniff is given "benevolence" as another of his many attributes (MC, p. 681). I suspect that Dickens has re-created in Pecksniff a counterfeit Pickwick—who, after all, did devote most of his life "to the pursuit of wealth" (PP, p. 796). In the process of his creation, Dickens may have discovered how easy it is to counterfeit such simple, effortless virtues as "blandness" and "benevolence." In the end, Mr. Pickwick becomes Mr. Podsnap.

Tom's Pecksniff, had ceased to exist, but that he had never existed" (MC, p. 493); then "There was no Pecksniff; there had never been a Pecksniff" (MC, p. 502); "But there was no Pecksniff; there had never been a Pecksniff, and the unreality of Pecksniff extended itself to [his] chamber" (MC, p. 502); "Pecksniff had gone out of the world—had never been in it" (MC, p. 505). What all this means is that "the substantial Pecksniff of [Tom's] heart [has] melted away" (MC, p. 556)—and that Dickens's concern with the real substance of the world has led him now to test the characters who grow out of it by the same substantial standards. Evil exists in the novel; and Dickens's method of characterization together with his environmental bias makes the relationship between the world and its characters a metaphysical one: characters seem to be "begotten of the slime from which they sprung, by the hot sun that burnt them up" (MC, p. 377)—to use one of Dickens's descriptions of the growth in Eden. There is a metaphysical relationship between moral character and being. In the metaphysics of the novel, Pecksniff, a false man, does not exist. This makes Mark wonder of Pecksniff "if he had ever been alive in all his life, worth mentioning" (MC, p. 658), and Martin can confront his grandfather in Pecksniff's room as though Pecksniff were not there: "he evinced no knowledge whatever of that gentleman's presence or existence. . . . there might have been nothing in his place save empty air" (MC, p. 666). Pecksniff speaks, and "Martin looked as steadily at his grandfather as if there had been a dead silence all this time" (MC, p. 669).

This concern with the metaphysical aspect of character does not end with Pecksniff. Early in the novel Pecksniff calls Mr. Chuffey—erroneously, as it turns out[9]—"metaphysically . . . a dummy" (MC, p. 302). Earlier, he has given us a false lead by defining part of the "very essence" of Martin's and Tom's char-

---

9. Unconvincingly, Dickens wakes Mr. Chuffey up to life in the scene of Jonas's discovery. Mr. Chuffey plays Mr. Micawber's part as well as Mr. Dick's to John Westlock's Tommy Traddles and Jonas's Heep.

acters as taking "a pleasure in patronizing, and . . . in being pa-
tronized" (MC, p. 100). As long as Tom is under the influence of
Pecksniff, he has no character, and no identity. Thus, when he
tries to write "a little description of [him]self" (MC, p. 601)
after leaving Pecksniff, he can get no further than "A respectable
young man, aged thirty-five" (MC, p. 603).

As happens so often in Dickens, an idea becomes an obsession.
Martin Chuzzlewit becomes a novel about existence and nonexistence, and thus not the moral "exhibition" of "Selfishness" that
Dickens said he had written. Sairey Gamp has her nonexistent friend, Mrs. Harris. Nadgett, the spy, is so secret that "even
what he was, was a secret," and it seems "as if he really didn't
know the secret himself" (MC, p. 497). He also has a friend who
doesn't exist, "the man who never came" (MC, p. 590). Bailey
junior has trouble with his many names (MC, p. 142); Montague
Tigg "change[s] his name, and change[s] his outward surface,"
and Montague Tigg becomes Tigg Montague, but "still it [is]
Tigg" (MC, p. 429). When Ruth Pinch makes her first beef-steak
pudding, the very existence of the beef comes into question: "We
can't cook it all to nothing," says Ruth (MC, p. 600). And Tom
says of the pudding itself, "I may as well call it that, till it proves
to be something else" (MC, p. 602).

Mark, who is the model character for the novel, metaphysically describes himself: "a Werb is a word as signifies to be, to do,
to suffer . . . and if there's a Werb alive, I'm it" (MC, p. 733).[10]
In the end of the novel, Mark announces the redefinition of the
Blue Dragon, and gives it a new identity: "the Blue Dragon will
be con-werted into the Jolly Tapley. A sign of my own inwention.
Wery new, conwivial, and expressive" (MC, p. 870). This sign

---

10. John Westlock is also a sort of model character, for Martin's benefit. He
reaches his majority and comes into his property, but still is conscious of being
in a state of "becoming" as he seeks his maturity. When Tom Pinch says, "so
you really are a gentleman at last, John," he answers, "Trying to be, Tom; trying
to be. . . . There is no saying what I may turn out, in time" (MC, p. 202).

is the symbol of the new and honorable version of Eden: the good place in the real world.

3

The Jolly Tapley is itself a mythic sort of place, at the end of *Martin Chuzzlewit*. Indeed, it is hardly a place, in any ordinary geographical sense. Martin and Mrs. Lupin bring it into being first in London at the great party at the end of the novel, before taking it down to Wiltshire. But then *Martin Chuzzlewit* is not a novel one would call geographical in its particulars, and in this it is not a typically Dickensian novel. With the exception of Todger's, in that unknowable "labyrinth" of streets near the Monument, and Sairey Gamp's house on Kingsgate Street, and the combined business and residence of Arthur Chuzzlewit and Son "in a very narrow street somewhere behind the Post Office" (MC, p. 175), there is no particularized London geography in the novel —and two of these places are not so very particular. One doesn't get a sense of place in *Martin Chuzzlewit*, except for the generic place called "the world." And perhaps this is why its mythological and metaphoric "Eden," then, can become so real.

In *Dombey and Son* Dickens takes us back to "the wild wilderness of London (D&S, p. 667), and the novel is established in the context of that descriptive place, real and fabricated: Dombey's house is in the region between Portland Place and Byanstone Square; Mrs. Skewton's house is in Brook Street; Miss Tox and Major Bagstock live in Princess's Place; the Toodleses live in Staggs's Gardens, in Camden Town; both the Wooden Midshipman and Dombey and Son are in the Leadenhall vicinity; Brogley, the broker, keeps his shop nearby in Bishopsgate Street Without; Captain Cuttle lives in Brig Place; Captain Bunsby's ship is tied up in Ratcliffe; Mr. Perch lives in Ball's Pond, and drinks in the City at the King's Arms; John and Harriet Carker live off the old north road out of London; James Carker lives in Norwood;

Sir Barnet Skittles, M.P., lives in a villa at Fulham, on the Thames.

But despite this physical realization of the novel, *Dombey and Son* is not a novel concerned with the real world. It is a sentimental tale, premised on dreams and dreams-come-true. Like *The Old Curiosity Shop* and *Oliver Twist*, it is dependent upon the myth of a happy world hereafter for its resolution to the problems and pains of the here and now. Perhaps this comes about as a result of Dickens's not having a strong young man in the novel to grow up to the real world. Walter Gay should fit this role in *Dombey and Son*, but he is sent off to Barbados to earn his maturity through experience there. Paul Dombey doesn't grow up, and Mr. Toots, "a wealthy young gentleman, of good heart but inferior abilities" (D&S, p. xxiii), is not capable of any great maturity. Florence Dombey is another one of Dickens's pious young creatures who, in her piety, is outside the complications of maturity and reality; but in the absence of a young hero on the scene, she assumes an important role, and personifies the sentimentality of the novel. She is Paul's only friend, Toots's first love, Susan Nipper's vestal goddess, Edith Dombey's inspiration, faithful and forgiving daughter to her father, and innocent brother to Walter, who becomes her husband. Her loving influence humanizes young Paul; he is otherwise a strange and terrible child. She brings out what is called the best in Susan Nipper, though this best turns out to be the Nipper's tears rather than her natural strength. She awakens true feeling in Edith's heart—but then, in the end, plays pious with Edith, asking her to beg forgiveness of her father, and is wonderfully rebuffed. Dickens uses Florence as a foil to Dombey, too—she is all heart, he has none—and in the end makes her triumph, breaking the proud cold man and reducing him to penitent imbecility.

Florence is her worst in her relationship with Walter. Sol Gills and Captain Cuttle have great ambitious dreams for Walter from the beginning, generally represented by reference to Dick

Whittington; and on the occasion of Walter's rescuing Florence, Sol builds "a great many airy castles of the most fantastic architecture" (D&S, p. 79). But none of this dreaming distorts Walter —and Florence's love does. Afraid of the world he is creating, Dickens insists on innocence rather than experience. Thus Florence's sentimental innocence undermines Walter's boyish love for her, and turns their relationship into that of "brother" and "sister." When he departs to sea, she prays, "if you'll be a brother to me, Walter . . . I'll be your sister all my life, and think of you like that wherever we may be" (D&S, p. 264). When he returns to England, she takes up the same cry: "Dear brother! Show me some way through the world . . . protect and care for me as a sister" (D&S, p. 695). Walter knows what is happening to him through all of this: "Miss Dombey, in her guileless innocent heart, regards me as her adopted brother; but what would the guile and guilt of *my* heart be, if I pretended to believe that I had any right to approach her familiarly, in that character" (D&S, pp. 701-2)—and Walter can't even say in *what* character, in the character of her lover. She has Walter so subdued as a man that he can tell her, "Never, never, before Heaven, have I thought of you but as the single, bright, pure, blessed recollection of my boyhood and youth. . . . never shall I . . . regard your part in my life, but as something sacred" (D&S, p. 711). Finally, she proposes to him: "If you will take me for your wife, Walter, I will love you dearly" (D&S, p. 713)—and they have to live happily ever after. Florence's love is so strange that Susan Nipper cannot understand that it could mean marriage. She proposes to accompany Florence and Walter on their voyage, and Florence has to explain to her, "I am going to be his wife, to give him up my whole heart, and to live with him and die with him. . . . Why, Susan, dear, I love him" (D&S, p. 787).

Florence's love for her father finally destroys him; and I wonder if, in the future which isn't told, it might not destroy Walter, too. Certainly it destroys the real world in this novel, and the possibility of Walter's living in it. When they are married—Captain Cuttle innocently proposes as the text or reference for the event "Adam and Eve" (D&S, p. 796)—they "walk through the streets together," and never, says the narrator, "were they so far removed from all the world about them as to-day":

> It is a fair, warm summer morning, and the sun shines on them, as they walk towards the darkening mist that overspreads the City. Riches are uncovering in shops; jewels, gold and silver flash in the goldsmith's sunny windows; and great houses cast a stately shade upon them as they pass. But through the light, and through the shade, they go lovingly together, lost to everything around. (D&S, p. 806)

They are already out of this world. And as they sail out from London to make Walter's fortune, Florence has a vision "of love, eternal and illimitable, not bounded by the confines of this world, or by the end of time, but ranging still beyond the sea, beyond the sky, to the invisible country far away" (D&S, p. 871). They are sailing away to heaven!

Dickens's return to the myth of immortality in *Dombey and Son* is symptomatic of the failure of his faith in this life and the ability of his characters to deal with it successfully.[11] When Captain Cuttle hears that Walter's ship has surely sunk, he goes into a kind of "retirement" in Sol Gill's shop, consoling himself with weekly reference to the Sermon on the Mount and daily dreams of his own fabrication:

> In this retirement, the Captain . . . would sit smoking, and thinking of Florence and poor Walter, until they both seemed to his homely fancy to be dead, and to have passed away into eternal youth, the beautiful and innocent children of his first remembrance. (D&S, p. 543)

When little Paul dies (his death, like little Nell's, is carried out over a space of a hundred or more pages) Dickens submerges him

---

11. Dickens mocks the myth of immortality at Dombey's and Edith's marriage, when Cousin Feenix (Phoenix) "puts his noble name into a wrong place, and enrols himself as having been born that morning" (D&S, p. 444).

sentimentally in the saving waters of Christian promise. Paul's last words are: "Mama is like you, Floy. I know her by the face! But tell them that the print upon the stairs at school is not divine enough. The light about the head is shining on me as I go." And then the narrator prays:

> The old, old fashion—Death!
> Oh thank God, all you who see it, for that older fashion yet, of Immortality! And look upon us, angels of young children, with regards not quite estranged, when the swift river bears us to the ocean! (D&S, p. 226)

It is just weakness—self-indulgence on Dickens's part—that creates these scenes. Neither they nor their sentiments are integral or relevant to the better part of the novel. The "swift river [that] bears us to the ocean" is the same metaphoric euphemism Dickens used at Paul's mother's death, as she "drifted out upon the dark and unknown sea that rolls round all the world" (D&S, p. 10), and it is the fulfillment of the imagistic pattern that has foreshadowed Paul's death. Elsewhere, that same river is introduced, not just as a metaphor for a route out of life, with the emphasis on the escape—"How fast the river runs," says Paul; "it's very near the sea" (D&S, p. 225)—but as a metaphor for the journey through life, which takes us through or by so much more before we reach the sea:

> Florence hurried away in the advancing morning, and the strengthening sunshine, to the City. The roar soon grew more loud, the passengers more numerous, the shops more busy, until she was carried onward in a stream of life setting that way, and flowing, indifferently, past marts and mansions, prisons, churches, market-places, wealth, poverty, good, and evil, like the broad river side by side with it, awakened from its dreams of rushes, willows, and green moss, and rolling on, turbid and troubled, among the works and cares of men, to the deep sea. (D&S, p. 668)

But Florence is hardly the person to be making this journey; she is too apt to be "lost to everything around" (D&S, p. 806), too

likely not to notice the contradictions of "prisons, churches, market-places, wealth, poverty, good, and evil . . . among the works
and cares of men."

Of similar sentimental irrelevance is Dickens's response to
Harriet Carker's charity to Dombey. Earlier Harriet has been
pious—it is her character—in her charity to Alice Marwood, and
has been challenged in return by a voice from this world. "Heav-
en help and forgive you!" Harriet says to Alice, and Alice responds "Ah! Heaven help me and forgive me! . . . If man would
help some of us a little more, God would forgive us all the sooner
perhaps" (D&S, p. 482). Harriet learns very little from this encounter. Later, when she and her brother help Dombey—who is
easy to help, having been a rich man, and never having committed
the crime of poverty or the crimes that poverty breeds—Harriet
says that their act will "live in my thoughts, only as a new reason
for thankfulness to Heaven, and joy and pride in my brother"
(D&S, p. 819). Dickens's pious response to this holy sentiment
is: "Such a look of exultation there may be on Angels' faces,
when the one repentant sinner enters Heaven, among ninety-nine
just men" (D&S, p. 819). The text is irrelevant. Dombey has not
entered heaven, or even repented at this stage. And surely
Dickens doesn't mean that John Carker, long ago repentant for
his theft, has now purchased entry into heaven by paying gold to
Dombey?

Dickens cannot imagine an order for this world while dreaming of the next, though even in his dreams of the next world he
cannot escape his terribly real vision of the chaos of this one.
Paul's childhood dream (it is excusable as Paul's, but not as
Dickens's) was to pool all the Dombey financial resources, "never
try to get any more, go away into the country with my darling
Florence, have a beautiful garden, fields, and woods, and live
there with her all my life" (D&S, p. 190). But such innocent unreal places are impossible refuges from the world, which is, as
usual, very real. In the original Staggs's Gardens, where Paul's

nurse and her large family live, Dickens sets his typical vision of chaos. That "earthquake" of progress called the railroad, which Dickens doesn't fully trust, is attacking Camden Town:

> Houses were knocked down; streets broken through and stopped; deep pits and trenches dug in the ground; enormous heaps of earth and clay thrown up; buildings that were undermined and shaking propped by great beams of wood. Here, a chaos of carts, overthrown and jumbled together, lay topsy-turvy at the bottom of a steep unnatural hill; there, confused treasures of iron soaked and rusted in something that had accidentally become a pond. Everywhere were bridges that led nowhere; thoroughfares that were wholly impassable; Babel towers of chimneys, wanting half their height; temporary wooden houses and enclosures, in the most unlikely situations; carcasses of ragged tenements, and fragments of unfinished walls and arches, and piles of scaffolding, and wildernesses of bricks. . . . There were a hundred thousand shapes and substances of incompleteness, wildly mingled out of their places, upside down, burrowing in the earth, aspiring in the air, mouldering in the water, and unintelligible as any dream. (D&S, pp. 62-63)

In the midst of this chaotic "dire disorder" there is a dream "of civilisation and improvement" (D&S, p. 63). When the railroad is completed, "the old rotten summer-houses" and the "miserable waste ground, where the refuse-matter had been heaped of yore" are "swallowed up and gone," replaced by "palaces . . . and granite columns of gigantic girth open[ing] a vista to the railway world beyond" (D&S, pp. 217-218). The dream that makes this change is a dream for this world, and its accomplishment comes through work, not sentiment.

The railroad is one example. The world is in need of man's best dreams and his hardest work. London, "the greatest city in the universe" (D&S, p. 288), is describable in terms of "the hospitals, the churchyards, the prisons, the river, fever, madness, vice, and death" (D&S, p. 480); it needs new dreams to replace the "rotten banks of religion, patriotism, virtue, honor" (D&S, p. 812). London is a "labyrinth' '(D&S, p. 792) again, a "wilderness" (D&S,

pp. 508, 667), a "world of odious sights" (D&S, p. 647), which it will take hard work to change. Dickens warns that "millions of immortal creatures have no other world on earth" (D&S, p. 697), and in that warning is Dickens's temptation—to which he has already submitted in this novel—to take his dreams out of this world, and wish all happiness and order immortally into the next. The "innocent" Mr. Toots cries:

> "Oh, upon my word and honour . . . a most wretched sort of affair this world is! Somebody's always dying, or going and doing something uncomfortable in it. I'm sure I never should have looked forward so much, to coming into my property, if I had known this. I never saw such a world. It's a great deal worse than Blimber's." (D&S, p. 462)

There are three additional but smaller symbolic worlds in *Dombey and Son* which exist in relation to the chaos and the dream. Sol Gills's little house, where the more honorable dreams of the novel were born, becomes in the end the firm of Gills and Cuttle; and of Sol's handicraft, which was for so many years useless, for lack of custom, there is a myth that it was not "behind the time," but "in truth, a little before it, and had to wait the fulness of the time and the design" (D&S, p. 874). The Captain, who has been a minor benevolent man with his watch, teaspoons, and sugar-tongs, is allowed in the end "a fiction, . . . which is better than any reality," that the Wooden Midshipman is important "to the commerce and navigation of the country" (D&S, pp. 874-75). This is not sentiment, but healthy comedy. Dickens can admit that Sol's handiwork alone will not enable us to navigate the ship of England—or the world—to "the fullness of the time and the design." But these two old bachelors have worked hard and done good, and they deserve, perhaps, these pleasant dreams. They are better dreams at any rate than heaven.

The second minor symbolic world is the house of Dombey, the "wilderness of a home" where Florence lives, and "bloom[s] . . . like the king's fair daughter in the story" (D&S, p. 320). Florence's blooming survival is another "principle of Good" projection; but the house of Dombey is real in fact and in symbol. The house is cold, and dark, and blank. It changes, temporarily, when Edith comes. It is artificially warmed and brightened—with money, but not with love. After Edith's elopement with James Carker the house reverts to its earlier aspect, and becomes "such a ruin that the rats have fled" (D&S, p. 837).

The third minor symbolic world is that which surrounds John and Harriet Carker's little house north of London. It stands in the midst of a "blighted country," with "a few tall chimneys belching smoke all day and night . . . where the fences tumble down, and where the dusty nettles grow" (D&S, p. 472). There is a "frowzy and uneven patch of ground . . . before their house, which had once (and not long ago) been a pleasant meadow, and was now a very waste, with a disorderly crop of beginnings of mean houses, rising out of the rubbish, as if they had been unskillfully sown there" (D&S, p. 474). The image is that of the ironic progress of civilization, back through Eden towards the aboriginal chaos. John and Harriet are, like Florence, symbolic good people—a brother-sister "family"—and they work to reclaim the world from waste in their humble ways. Their house is "a poor, small house, barely and sparely furnished, but very clean; and there is even an attempt to decorate it, shown in the homely flowers trained about the porch and in the narrow garden" (D&S, p. 472). The problem with John and Harriet is that they are too good to be true, too good to do anything more than set unbelievable sentimental examples for the rest of us. They are not remaking the world; rather, they are prettying up their own front yard, and Dickens is pretending that this is the beginning of universal urban renewal.

Not only do the Carkers set this incredibly good example of changing and improving their environment, they also are examples of personal change as well. John is a man who has recovered from an earlier mistake and lives now in this penitential retreat.

Harriet says to Mr. Morfin, who is another minor benevolent man and a bachelor (D&S, pp. 815-16), that her brother "was an altered man when he did wrong. . . . He is an altered man again, and is his true self now" (D&S, p. 477). The change, she says, is "a metaphysical sort of thing" (D&S, p. 477). However seriously intended this theory of change is here, it is not convincing, because of the sentimentality and the piety. The nonexistence of Dombey that follows his hitting Florence—"There was no such Being in the world" (D&S, p. 681)—is not convincing either, partly because of Florence's piety: "She only knew that she had no Father upon earth, and she said so, many times, with her suppliant head hidden from all, but her Father who was in Heaven" (D&S, p. 681). This idea worked in *Martin Chuzzlewit*, in the denial of Pecksniff, but as an idea it was legitimate and valid there. Something similar works triumphantly in *David Copperfield*, when Miss Betsey ignores the existence of Miss Murdstone in chapter 14. Here, the great comic exposure of Mrs. Skewton is much more successful. Metaphysically she is the ancestor of Mr. Turveydrop and Lady Tippins. Her gesture of forgetful speech mocks the dream of "Eden," "the garden of what's-its-name" (D&S, p. 287), the "what's-his-name" of "seclusion and contemplation" which Edith reminds her is called "Paradise" (D&S, p. 288). And as love is substance in Dickens's world, Mrs. Skewton speaks with ironic metaphysical eloquence of "gratitude, and natural whats-its-name, and all the rest of it," and of "affection and et cetera" (D&S, p. 575).[12]

As comedy—even as satire—*Dombey and Son* is successful; as a serious novel, however, it is not. Dickens's comic genius—

---

12. This gesture appears twice in *Martin Chuzzlewit*. Montague Tigg speaks of going "to that what's-his-name from which no thingumbob comes back" (MC, p. 47), and Jonas encourages his old father to die soon with the suggestion that he "hide [his] head in the what-you-may-call-it" (MC, p. 299). Considering Mrs. Skewton's use of this technique of non-speech, it is interesting that both Tigg and Jonas use it to refer to death. Tigg also refers to "Whittington, afterwards thrice Lord Mayor of London" (MC, p. 101).

which is in its own way serious—was at work in the creation of Mrs. Skewton, Joe Bagstock (who fabricates an identity out of his many names), Cousin Feenix, Miss Tox, Mr. and Mrs. Chick, Susan Nipper, Mr. Toots (who can get nobody's name right, and has cards to keep track of his own), Sol Gills, Captain Cuttle, and even Walter Gay. But the representations of evil—James Carker, Alice Marwood, and Mrs. Brown—are melodramatic. The good conceptions of Dombey and Edith and the tension of their complex conflict are lost amid these sentimental distractions. Perhaps a novel concerned just or primarily with Dombey and Edith would have been impossible for Dickens to write. Such a novel would mean Dickens's assuming a much more limited and pessimistic realism than suited him. They are both too old—and Dombey too cold, like ice, and Edith too hard, like stone—to change. They would fit a petrifying mythology centering on the image of Lot's immutable stone wife better than one which works out of the dynamic Genesis myths of change and revolution.

3

DAVID COPPERFIELD

O F ALL DICKENS'S NOVELS, *David Copperfield* IS THE MOST intimately concerned with that finally unmanageable problem, both real and mythic, of ordering a disordered world. In examining this disorder, it includes in its critical focus a representative list of institutions, from school, church, and government to the basic social institution, the family. The larger purpose of the novel transcends this criticism, however, and becomes almost a model working out of Dickens's resolution to the incontrovertible fact of our chaos. In this sense, *David Copperfield* is the most positive of all Dickens's novels, and perhaps his most important work for himself and for us.

Dickens's general thesis, propounded in novel after novel, is that love, which cannot be institutionalized, is the only force capable of ordering this world. In various novels, including both *Pickwick Papers* and *Our Mutual Friend*, there are vain attempts to organize love through the agency of the law. In *Hard Times* Mrs. Gradgrind discovers on her deathbed that "there is something—not an Ology at all—that your father has missed, or forgotten, Louisa" (HT, p. 199). As Mr. Sleary says, love has "a way of [its] own of calculating or not calculating" (HT, p. 293). For

Dickens, the "bright old song" is right which says "that oh, 'tis love, 'tis love, 'tis love, that makes the world go round" (OMF, p. 671).

But the world goes round even in the absence of love, and keeps spinning and spinning down into chaos—this is the problem for Dickens. In the early novels he tries to ignore it; in the later ones he keeps reminding himself of it. Miss Flite announces in *Bleak House* that order, which is the archetypal perfection of love, will come only "on the Day of Judgment" (BH, p. 33). In *Hard Times* Stephen Blackpool can't foresee the world's being governed by love, by the rule of "drawin' nigh to folk, wi' kindness and patience," until "the sun turns t' ice . . . till God's work is onmade" (HT, p. 151). This kind of final universal resolution does not take place at the end of a Dickens novel, of course; though we can expect to find a new beginning made, both mythically and realistically, we never actually get to the end of the world, to Judgment Day. As I have argued, Dickens's solution in the early novels is to situate those new beginnings in little pockets of love which ignore the old, ruined world about them. He lets the good people establish for themselves retreats in the midst of the greater chaos where they will live on their love for each other, ignoring that pervasive calamity which is the world at large. In *David Copperfield*, however, Dickens finds an alternative to his retreat solution, which changes all the rest of his fiction.

It is obvious from the beginning of Dickens's career that the pocket of love solution is not the right one. Mr. Pickwick determines "on retiring to some quiet pretty neighborhood in the vicinity of London," trusting that he "may yet live to spend many quiet years in peaceful retirement." Mr. Pickwick calls the place his "little retreat," and from it he announces the "dissolution" of the Pickwick Club (PP, p. 796). The happiness he finds in this retirement from the world is promised a continuance which, in the last words of the novel, "nothing but death will terminate"

(PP, p. 801). The world of experience, as discovered by the adventuring Pickwickians, is already dead in the fact of Mr. Pickwick's retreat; and that life being gone, there is little of healthy life left. The novel is, fully, *The Posthumous Papers of the Pickwick Club.*

Oliver Twist suffers similarly in its conclusion. In the final chapter, the narrator tries to generate a future for his good people by means of wishful meditation:

> And now, the hand that traces these words, falters, as it approaches the conclusion of its task; and would weave, for a little longer space, the threads of these adventures.
> I would fain linger yet with a few of those among whom I have so long moved, and share their happiness by endeavoring to depict it. I would show Rose Maylie in the bloom and grace of early womanhood. . . . I would paint her and her dead sister's child happy in their love for one another, and passing whole hours together in picturing the friends whom they had so sadly lost. (OT, pp. 414-15)

The hiding place for happiness here seems to be in the memories of the past, among the dead rather than among the living. This conclusion is unsatisfactory, not just because it is sentimental, but because it violates life by ignoring it. In *David Copperfield* Dickens attempts to find—or finds and attempts to accept—a much greater and more satisfactory solution. He finds this solution primarily in the careers of Tommy Traddles and David himself, each of whom orders reality, not by changing or reforming it, but by comprehending and accepting it in all its complexity. At the end of the novel Traddles is to become a judge; David is a novelist.

There are different kinds of order—physical, for example, and mental, or real and imaginary. The world is in a state of chaos, physically, really; and it cannot be converted to order overnight, or by the concerted goodness and even the hard work of several good men. The effort can be begun, of course—must be begun. But what it takes to begin this impossible task is courage, which comes only with a critical but sympathetic understanding of the whole problem. Understanding requires mental—"rational" is the word Miss Betsy uses (DC, p. 274)—and imaginative activity. Understanding is itself a kind of order, finally, the kind of order that lets us see what the whole problem of chaos really is.

The problem of finding and reestablishing order is a qualitative one in *David Copperfield*, involving the determination of innocence and experience. With the exception of David himself, the good people of the novel all insist on their innocence; all except David and Traddles try, initially, to refuse or refute experience, making their worlds thus exclusive and selective. In denying the existence of the larger, pervasive reality of evil—natural as well as human—they establish for themselves precarious and difficult situations. Their love, then, becomes restrictive and isolationist, and that larger, responsible love which would establish itself critically and creatively in the world, however painful this might be, is denied.

The basic unit of love and order, the family, is almost nonexistent in *David Copperfield*, and it is against this symbolically significant disadvantage that the characters all react. David himself is a posthumous child, and soon an orphan. Steerforth has no father, and Traddles is an orphan; Ham and Little Emily are orphans, and Mrs. Gummidge is a widow. Agnes Wickfield has no mother, Annie Strong no father; Dora Spenlow's mother is dead, and her father dies midway through the novel. Mr. Dick has been mistreated and deserted by his family, and lives with Miss Betsey, who is divorced. Uriah Heep's father is dead, Sophy Crewler's mother dies, and Martha, the Yarmouth prostitute, is an orphan. The only unbroken family unit in the novel is that of the Micawbers, which struggles against its own chaotic social incompetence and chronic moral ineptitude to stay whole; and when they move to Plymouth, they leave behind an orphan servant to be "disbanded" (DC, p. 174), a metaphysical malapropism for the breaking up of a home.

In order to overcome the disadvantage of orphanage and to make contact again beyond its symbolic isolation the characters must create new orders, new forms in which to live. The largest of these orders and forms are Traddles's, in marriage and in his career as a lawyer, and David's, in his adjustment and organization of the whole "family" of the novel in the last chapter, and in his work as a novelist, as a creative artist. What we see of the orders by which the other characters live we see through David's imaginative eye; and he represents each of these attempts at order in terms of one or another of the myths which Dickens himself has used in his earlier novels to try to resolve the problem of chaos.

Mr. Peggotty tries to establish order for Ham, Emily, Mrs. Gummidge, and himself in the houseboat, making for them all an artificial home on the edge of "the great dull waste" of Yarmouth. The first time David visits there he looks out "over the wilderness, and away at the sea, and away at the river, but no house could *I* make out. There was a black barge, or some other kind of super-annuated boat, not far off, high and dry on the ground" (DC, p. 29). This unimposing Noah's Ark—such is the obvious translation for that "other kind of super-annuated boat"—is set up by Mr. Peggotty in opposition to the tides of universal chaos, and seems to young David, once he knows the place, to be "the most delicious retreat that the imagination of man could conceive" (DC, p. 32). It is only a retreat, however, and it seems safe only to that kind of romantic or childish imagination which foresees nothing but the best of fortunes. David innocently asks Mr. Peggotty if he gave his "son the name of Ham, because [he] lived in a sort of ark" (DC, p. 32). But Mr. Peggotty is not really Noah, and Ham, Noah's son, has no father in this world. Mr. Peggotty is a benevolent bachelor, not a mythological savior; and his "sort of ark" is not protection enough from the real world.[1]

---

1. Noah's Ark appears one other time by name, as David sees some boats at

As both David and Steerforth notice on the night of Steerforth's first visit to Yarmouth, the reality of the wilderness world threatens constantly to destroy Mr. Peggotty's simple refuge:

> "This is a wild kind of place, Steerforth, is it not?"
> "Dismal enough in the dark," he said: "and the sea roars as if it were hungry for us. Is that the boat, where I see a light yonder?" (DC, p. 311)

When David returns the next time, on the occasion of Little Emily's disappearance, it is again "a wild night" in the universe, and David has to do "a little floundering across the sand, which was heavy," to get to the houseboat and its light (DC, p. 448). The retreat is a haven, or a lighthouse, perched precariously on shifting sands, surrounded by troubled seas. With the seduction of Emily the retreat fails, and the experiment is ruined. Mr. Peggotty sets out to retrieve Emily, but upon recovering her realizes that he cannot now reestablish the innocent world which has been, and thus the little houseboat is abandoned. The tides of the world have proved too strong; the houseboat-ark is drowned, and Mr. Peggotty takes what is left of his broken family and escapes to never-never land, in Australia. As Mr. Peggotty, Emily, Mrs. Gummidge, and Martha leave, the storm comes again, destroying Ham, Steerforth, and the empty house itself. David finds Steerforth's body on the beach, "on the part where [Emily] and I had looked for shells, two children—on that part of it where some lighter fragments of the old boat, blown down last night, had been scattered by the wind—among the ruins of the home he had wronged" (DC, p. 795).

Experience destroys the houseboat; those of its former inhabitants who escape retreat to Australia, a minor heaven or haven, an unknown place where what should have been can now be, in

---

Chatham "roofed like Noah's arks" (DC, p. 183) on his runaway trip to Miss Betsey's private Eden at Dover.

what pretends to be this life. It is as though Eden has been reestablished. The intrusion of such unreality on the novel is an indication of Dickens's continuing inability to resolve happily and at the same time honestly that which he so much wanted to resolve. Faced with a calamitous world, Dickens's innocents can only be saved by being given "retreats" again; this is the best the imagination can create without completely denying the thesis of experience.

David describes his own technique as a novelist as the "blending of experience and imagination" (DC, p. 665), and generally this is Dickens's technique as well. Unfortunately, even in this most autobiographically based of his novels, Dickens does not always remain as true to his principles as David the novelist seems to, and the realism and moral integrity of his art are sometimes compromised by romantic falsification. The falsification of reality for the sake of innocence is not only a constant temptation for Dickens, it is also the constant endeavor of various characters in the novel. This endeavor is what must be considered first here in order to bring David's response to the difficulties of reality into better focus. The range of the characters' culpability for this unwise insistence upon innocence runs from the positive and only half-comic guilt of Micawber to the comic goodness of Traddles, which ends in his being touted for a judgeship.

Micawber, kinsman to Harold Skimpole in *Bleak House*, reveals the more serious side of the problem of innocence. Micawber is irresponsible, and is in fact a thief, although the one thing he seems to use money for is the punch which generates good fellowship.[2] Mrs. Micawber insists that it is society's duty to employ her husband, and society's responsibility to find a proper use for his talents; one knows, however, that although society is almost always wrong in Dickens's fiction, the Micawbers are at

---

2. "I never saw a man," writes David, "so thoroughly enjoy himself amid the fragrance of lemon-peel and sugar, the odour of burning rum, and the steam of boiling water, as Mr. Micawber did" (DC, p. 412).

fault here, too. The situation becomes so morally complex for Dickens that in order to resolve Micawber in the novel's London he would have to readjust his whole world, and establish David and Micawber as supports for each other, Micawber becoming the father David wants, and David becoming the child-father Micawber needs. Rather than do this (which would change the focus of the novel entirely) Dickens sends the Micawber family, with Mr. Peggotty and his group, to Australia. There everything works out as it should have in this world, if only life were simple. It is as though Micawber has been read out of the novel's real world and into a storybook world of mythical innocence.

This quest for continuing innocence all begins, in a way, with storybooks: with young David reading *Tom Jones* as "a child's Tom Jones, a harmless creature" (DC, p. 56), with Peggotty insisting from the beginning of the novel until its end on the crocodile book, refusing to let that earlier, innocent world die. Although Peggotty doesn't understand the story about the crocodiles very well—"She had a cloudy impression . . . that they were a sort of vegetable" (DC, p. 16)—and isn't even "quite right in the name" of the things (DC, p. 17); still the story is a proper one for its purpose: the "monsters" "hatch" and populate the world, and then must be fought and defeated, of course, by the "natives" (DC, p. 18). In this storybook version of experience the conflict is falsified for the sake of sentimental innocence, and the natives all live happily ever after.

Young David is constantly meeting such attempts as Peggotty's to exorcise the world of its evil. Miss Betsey Trotwood responds to the mistake of her early marriage by withdrawing from the world and establishing for herself a retreat at Dover where she attempts to reconstruct her own private Eden, much restricted and diminished, but pure. Almost immediately upon David's arrival at Dover she is forced to do battle with the invading reality which constantly threatens to defile that ideal place. At the sight of the intruders she "became in one moment rigid with indignation, and had hardly voice to cry out, 'Janet! Donkeys!' "

David Copperfield

Upon which, Janet . . . darted out on a little piece of green in front, and warned off two saddle donkeys, lady-ridden, that had presumed to set hoof upon it; while my aunt, rushing out of the house, seized the bridle of a third animal laden with a bestriding child, turned him, led him forth from those sacred precincts, and boxed the ears of the unlucky urchin in attendance who had dared to profane that hallowed ground. (DC, pp. 194-95)

The narrator continues: "The one great outrage of her life, demanding to be constantly avenged, was the passage of a donkey over that immaculate spot" (DC, p. 195).

Miss Betsy's little Eden symbolizes her retreat from life. She has been wronged in marriage and has been unable to face life since. She has withdrawn, and reassumed her maiden name—which is like going back in time "before the Fall." Through her experience with David, however, Miss Betsey is drawn back into life, back into the real world. In returning she compromises her defensive idealism and begins to measure the world according to the wise, sad rule of reality. There are no immaculate green spots in this world; and at its center, in London, as Miss Betsey herself says, the only thing "genuine" is "the dirt" (DC, p. 345). In the end David reports that she "allowed [his] horse on the forbidden ground, but had not yet relented at all toward the donkeys" (DC, p. 858). Miss Betsey comes back to the real world now, and can deal with the fact of evil better than she could before. Still, no donkeys are allowed—and the donkeys, obviously, are evil.[3]

Mr. Dick's response to this disorderly world is one of the most interesting, most complex, and most important, metaphorically and thematically, in the novel. The realization of Dick as a character—and as a writer—gives us one side of Dickens himself. When David first visits Mr. Dick's room as a boy, Dick is at work on the Memorial, and David has "ample leave to observe the large paper kite in the corner [and] the confusion of bundles of

---

3. Mr. Chillup, the old doctor, never gains this kind of understanding. Late in the novel he remarks to David, "I *don't* find authority for Mr. and Miss Murdstone in the New Testament" (DC, p. 834).

manuscript" (DC, p. 202). Dick then looks up, greets David
cryptically as "Phoebus," and asks:

> "How does the world go? I'll tell you what," he added, in a lower
> tone, "I shouldn't wish it to be mentioned, but it's a"—here he beck-
> oned to me, and put his lips close to my ear—"it's a mad world. Mad as
> Bedlam, boy!" (DC, p. 202)

Dick recognizes David both as an artist and as a son in that initial
address; and he sees that, like Keats's Apollo in the first *Hype-
rion*, the young David needs to be instructed in the experience of
the world if he is to fulfill his destiny in art. According to Miss
Betsey, Dick's reason for calling the world mad is his own family situation. His brother has tried to institutionalize him and his
sister has married a cruel man who mistreats her. Dick, a compassionate, loving creature, is thrown into a fever by these events, the
consequence of which is that oppression which is expressed in the
metaphorical intrusion of King Charles's head into his life.
"That's his allegorical way of expressing it," Miss Betsey says;
"He connects his illness with great disturbances and agitation,
naturally, and that's the figure, or the simile, or whatever it's
called, which he chooses to use" (DC, p. 205).

Dick speaks his emphatic best in the terms of this metaphor.
He is writing a "Memorial," petitioning the Crown for relief
from the grief of his particular family situation. Miss Betsey tells
young David that "he is memorializing the Lord Chancellor or
the Lord Somebody or other—one of those people, at all events,
who are paid to *be* memorialized—about his affairs" (DC, p.
205). But to memorialize "the Lord Somebody or other" is to
memorialize God; and thus Dick's memorial is much more than
Miss Betsey assumes it to be. Dick is complaining about the general state of man, and the Memorial is the document which attempts to describe the "Mad as Bedlam" world which Dick sees.
King Charles's head is the symbolic expression of Dick's complaint about this "Mad as Bedlam" world, and he says it over

and over, impetuously, compulsively, unable to wait for the logic and rhetoric of exposition.

When Miss Betsey loses her fortune, Mr. Dick is put to work to earn money. He tries first to aid his protector with his innocence— "if I could exert myself, Mr. Traddles," Dick says; "if I could beat a drum—or blow anything!" (DC, p. 528)—but innocence will not solve the world's and Miss Betsey's problems. It seems that only something like Carlylean endeavor will do it; and so Mr. Dick is put to work being useful, copying legal documents which Traddles procures for him to earn silver sixpences. Dick produces his copies in an orderly fashion only by keeping King Charles's head out of them, which he accomplishes by writing that grievance over and over into an old copy of the Memorial, exorcising in this way the evil he sees in the world until he becomes so involved in the positive productive activity of copying that he "postpone[s] the Memorial to a more convenient time" (DC, p. 529). As the novel draws to its close, Miss Betsey, her fortune recovered, informs David that Dick now "incessantly occupied himself in copying everything he could lay his hands on, and kept King Charles the First at a respectful distance by that semblance of employment" (DC, p. 836). In the last chapter, which finally brings the time of the story into the present tense time of its writing, Dick is seen as "an old man, making giant kites, and gazing at them in the air, with a delight for which there are no words" (DC, p. 874).

When David was a small boy living at Miss Betsey's house, his first visit to Mr. Dick's room showed him a kite "as much as seven feet high." As David looked at the kite, he saw "that it was covered with manuscript, very closely and laboriously written; but so plainly, that as I looked along the lines, I thought I saw some allusion to King Charles the First's head again, in one or two places" (DC, p. 203). That first kite of Dick's was used to memorialize God, and to get rid of that evil which Dick simply could not comprehend: " 'There's plenty of string,' said Mr.

Dick, 'and when it flies high, it takes the facts a long way' " (DC, p. 203). In the end, the people of the novel have resolved their various difficulties with the world, and Dick flies what seem to be blank kites up to heaven. There is still a Memorial to be written, however; the world is not suddenly or at last perfect. But Dick has given over the job of "memorializing" to David, the artist, who presumably can handle the job without losing his sanity, without resorting to King Charles's head.

For Dick, of course, the world now is a satisfactory place. He has David's children to play with, and flies "giant kites" for them. He tells David that the Memorial—his Memorial—belongs to that future when he will "have nothing else to do" (DC, p. 875). Dick has learned to live with the world by working in it and busying himself with it. Carlyle, it seems, was right. The lesson Mr. Dick has learned is the same lesson that is taught to Miss Betsey: one cannot retire from the world, and either try from that retirement to change it or expect others to change it for one. Perhaps this is the lesson that Dickens is trying to learn, also, through his alter ego David. Innocence is not experience; innocence is both inadequate and irresponsible in the formation of order.[4]

Peggotty is the only character who is allowed to retain her faith in innocence—at least in David's childhood and that particular innocence—and the crocodile book is in her pocket still in the final chapter. To be allowed to retain that past is Peggotty's reward for her goodness, her love, and her strength, and for giving generously of these when others needed her support. David, however, has grown beyond her living memories, and has to look far back to see himself as he was then: "I find it very curious to see my own infant face, looking up at me from the Crocodile stories" (DC, p. 874). He has taken and continues to take Miss Betsey's

---

4. One of the meanings of Harold Skimpole in *Bleak House* is related to this. Through him Dickens settles for himself the make-believe that innocence and childishness are legitimate responses to the world.

important advice: "It's in vain, Trot, to recall the past, unless it works some influence upon the present" (DC, p. 347).

Agnes, like Peggotty, would keep the innocent past if she could: "I have found a pleasure," she tells David toward the novel's end, "in keeping everything as it used to be when we were children. For we were very happy then, I think" (DC, p. 840). But living in the past is not the way to make a future, nor is it the way to order life. Finally Agnes is required to give up the past, in which her relation to David was that of "good angel," of "brother," and become his "trew wife," as Mr. Peggotty calls her (DC, p. 866), "the real heroine," as Dickens described her in his notes for the novel.[5] What Miss Betsey calls the important "influence" of that surrendered past—with its happiness and love—is what is matured in the achieved future of the end of the novel.

Miss Betsey, Mr. Dick, and Agnes are all three forced to accept more of reality than they had bargained for. They are all required to come into the world of the real present in order to survive: Miss Betsey from her private Eden, Mr. Dick from his dream of divine intervention to resolve this mess, and Agnes from her sentimental retreat into the past of childhood. Dr. Strong, the teacher and lexicographer, achieves both peace and some sort of productivity for himself in a similar fashion. It is only by coming to terms with his own affairs and seeing the reality of his relationship with his wife and her family, that he can settle down peacefully to his task of ordering all of the world by cataloging and defining its symbols. At the end of the novel he is "labouring at his Dictionary (somewhere about the letter D), and happy in his wife and home" (DC, p. 876).[6]

---

5. John Butt and Kathleen Tillotson, *Dickens at Work* (Fair Lawn, New Jersey, 1958), p. 128. The problem of Agnes's inadequacy as a character is not germane here; however, it is her innocence that causes Dickens to create her as but David's "good angel," "pointing upward"—unless it is David, not Dickens, who cannot see her realistically.
6. Dr. Strong's plan for ordering the whole of reality by ordering its lan-

Only two characters in the novel consistently approach the world with total honesty and courage, and in the end they alone seem capable of leading it. In the end they alone seem to have succeeded in actually mastering it and understanding its full complexity. One, Tommy Traddles, will become a judge. The other, David, is a novelist, an artist. And although Tommy's judgeship is but prospective at the end and David's career as an artist is played down throughout the novel, there are no work or professional assignments in all of Dickens's fiction more significant than these two. David is Dickens's only novelist—although there is an earlier approximation of the artist in the career of young Martin Chuzzlewit as an architect, and Mr. Pickwick was a journalist of sorts. Traddles has the company of but Mortimer Lightwood and Eugene Wrayburn from among Dickens's dozens of legal figures as successful and sympathetically drawn lawyers.

At Salem School Tommy takes out his frustration in tears and skeleton-drawing every time he is abused by Mr. Creakle, every time injustice and disorder impinge upon his idealized conception of the world. He remains an innocent and a sort of idealist throughout the novel, and never, as far as one knows, does he give up his doodling. He literally "draws" the awful reality of the world out of himself onto scraps of paper. Still, Traddles learns and accepts the lessons of experience, though experience does not change him. He maintains his essential innocence; his response to evil in the world never ceases to be compassionate and humanitarian, built on selfless understanding and charity.

---

guage alphabetically is destined to fall far short of completion—largely because it is a mythic act, and not merely dictionary-making. Just as love and order will be fulfilled in this world only on "the Day of Judgment" in *Bleak House*, only "when the sun turns t' ice" in *Hard Times*, so the head-boy's calculation "of the time this Dictionary would take in completing, on the Doctor's plan, and at the Doctor's rate of going" is "that it might be done in one thousand six hundred and forty-nine years counting from the Doctor's last, or sixty-second birthday" (DC, pp. 237-38). Along with Mr. Dick and David, Dr. Strong is still another aspect of the personal and professional Charles Dickens, seeking a way to reorder the world through the use of words.

He achieves something like a Blakean "higher innocence," it seems; and it may well be in response to just this in his character that Dickens establishes Tommy's prospects for a judgeship. In the end Traddles is knowing and well informed about the world, but uncorrupted by this experience. He will order the world in the only legitimate and honest way possible, by simply accepting it as it is, with love.

David's career is quite different from Traddles's, and his calling is, for Dickens, the higher one.[7] In order to discover the meaning of his career we must look first at the full title of the novel, *The Personal History, Adventures, Experience, and Observation of David Copperfield the Younger.*[8] In a way, our calling the novel simply *David Copperfield* is like calling Joyce's first novel *Stephen Hero*. *A Portrait of the Artist as a Young Man* is a title that would begin to explain Dickens's novel in the same way that it begins to explain Joyce's. David Copperfield is a novelist. One of the points of difference between the character David and the narrator David is that the character David writes novels of social criticism, and is at work on such during the course of the story which the narrator writes, which is, of course, the novel we are reading, *David Copperfield*. The David who writes the novels of social criticism is writing Charles Dickens's career to this point; the David who writes *David Copperfield* seems to represent Dickens's ambition as an artist.

Agnes tells David the character late in the novel, "Your growing reputation and success enlarge your power of doing good;

---

7. One of Dickens's trial titles was "Mag's Diversions," "mag" being British slang for a chatterer, a talker, a magpie. The title finally chosen takes David's use of words much more seriously.
8. Cf. Mr. Pickwick's plan for "extending his travels, and consequently enlarging his sphere of observation, to the advancement of knowledge, and the diffusion of learning," and his instructions from the Pickwick Club to forward "authenticated accounts of their journeys and investigations, of their observations of character and manners, and of the whole of their adventures" (PP, pp. 1-2); and Martin Chuzzlewit's "enlarg[ing] his circle of acquaintance; increas[ing] his stock of wisdom; and [multiplying] his own experiences" (MC, p. 278).

and if I could spare my brother . . . perhaps the time could not" (DC, p. 843). Later, in his letter from Australia, Micawber addresses David as "the eminent author," and asserts the high seriousness of the art of fiction, claiming that the "inhabitants of Port Middlebay" read his novels "with delight, with entertainment, with instruction" (DC, p. 872). David the narrator, however, speaks but little of his occupation, and plays down the mention of his works: "When I refer to them, incidentally, it is only as a part of my progress" (DC, p. 690).

The story of David's "progress" is, in one sense, quite a simple one. As a child, David is required to relinquish his innocence, and the world which he meets beyond this innocence contains all of the evil which the novel describes. For David, time does not stand still, as it did momentarily in his childhood, in his first innocent infatuation with Emily: "The days sported by us," the narrator recalls, "as if Time had not grown up himself yet, but were a child too, and always at play" (DC, p. 37). Only in Eden was time a child; the real world ever since has been a world of change. So time goes on, and David goes to Salem School, to his mother's funeral, and to Murdstone and Grinby's; he goes through an acquaintance with the Micawbers and, as a consequence of that acquaintance, to pawnshops and to the King's Bench Prison. Finally, his boyhood experience, that first and most subjective part of his "Personal History," reaches its climax in his pilgrim's journey through seventy miles of the world to Dover. The narrator recreates David's consciousness of the experience which precipitated this journey on his first day at Dr. Strong's school: "I was so conscious of having passed through scenes of which they could have no knowledge, and of having acquired experience foreign to my age, appearance, and condition as one of them, that I half believed it was an imposture to come there as an ordinary little schoolboy" (DC, p. 228).

After his schooling is completed, David tries out the law as a profession, but gives it up under stress and never returns to it.

David Copperfield

He tries escape into childishness—in this novel it is called "Eden" (DC, p. 392), which is the same thing as "Fairyland" (DC, p. 396) and "a Fairy's bower" (DC, p. 543)—with Dora, and discovers not only that he is unhappy but that he and Dora are "corrupting" others through their "want of system and management" (DC, pp. 692, 694). Dora dies as a result of a miscarriage, and in the end of the novel David marries Agnes.

This accounting of David's "Personal History," however, is not the novel. Again, we must define the focus of the work, and to do so we must refer again to the full title. In the beginning of the novel our attention is directed toward the "Adventures" of young David because they are his, and David the narrator is telling us about himself as a child in the world. Later, our attention is redirected, and the narrator tells us to look at the world as David grew to look at it, and as it affected him. At this point we read, not of David the character's "Adventures," but of his "Observation," of the "Experience" which has made his point of view—which has made, indeed, his point of view as an artist. What holds the whole novel together is that everything in it belongs to David. The stories of the Peggottys, the Micawbers, Miss Betsey, Mr. Dick, and Dr. Strong are all parts of David's comprehension, which is why they have been analyzed here.

The two sides of David's "Experience" are, first, his "Personal History and Adventures," and second, his "Observation." His "Observation" includes all the various adventures and experiences of the other characters and sets of characters he meets, and his imaginative interpretation of them. In putting together both of these sides of his "Experience," David comes to an understanding of the world—an understanding, at least, of the large and representative world which this novel describes. It is this understanding and the activity of putting together by which the understanding is achieved, that is David's destiny, David's career as we know it. It is this destiny, then, that establishes the critical place or function in the novel of Miss Betsey, Mr. Dick, the Micawbers, the Peggottys, Steerforth, Littimer, Uriah Heep, Dora, Agnes, and all the rest.

David's destiny is not simply to marry Dora, and then to marry Agnes, and to live happily ever after. What he is required to do is comprehend reality, and in so doing order not only his own life but the world around him as well. David's destiny is the mythical ordering of his "Personal History, Adventures, Experience, and Observations." A more direct way of saying this is to say that David's destiny is the writing of *David Copperfield*, and that this work of his is finally the primary focus of the novel. David's destiny is dependent upon and formed from his understanding of the fates of all the other characters. The association is an intimate one, and David is involved dramatically, organically, personally, and psychologically in their lives. Finally, he *is* his understanding of and response to all these characters and in this he is an artist.

The narrator of *David Copperfield* is correct, initially, in his de-emphasis of his work as a novelist as a relevant matter for this story. The novels which David writes are not in themselves immediately important for *David Copperfield*; that he is a novelist, however, is of the utmost importance, as this gives us our best clue to understanding what the novel is about and what it achieves. As the novel draws toward its conclusion, David and his narrator become one person. Throughout the course of the story the narrator has recreated his own past, taking Miss Betsey's advice "to recall the past" only as "it works some influence upon the present" (DC, p. 347). He engages in what he calls "the blending of experience and imagination" (DC, p. 665) in order to recreate that past in a meaningful way. What he makes of it, of his "Personal History, Adventures, Experience, and Observation," is a comprehensible universe of experience, to which he gives the eponymous title, *David Copperfield*. The largest thing we can say of David is that he is, at this point, his novel; and in this he fulfills his destiny.

David Copperfield

In the end, as the two Davids merge into one, David writes this novel. In doing so he fulfills the purpose of the artist, to form order out of chaos, by making the larger world of experience meaningful. He is careful to change, exclude, or falsify none of the reality of the world he creates—and it is for this, for his comprehension and acceptance of his world as it is, that he is so important a character for Dickens.

If the answer to the old question about God's allowing evil to exist in the world is that God understands evil better than we do, and thus allows it, then the artist as a creator is also obliged to recognize the existence of evil, accept it, and understand it. This is not to say that evil must not be judged; Dickens, at any rate, frequently passes judgment upon the world, editorially. David's obligation, however, as Dickens conceives it, is to comprehend, not to judge; anything represented in its proper, full perspective will or should judge itself. Like Mr. Dick, Dickens is himself sometimes impatient with his readers; one of the achievements of David as a novelist is that, at least in this novel, he is never impatient. As a consequence of this, we can accept more easily the whole of the experience—without needing any "authority," for example, for Mr. Murdstone, and readily admitting to the triumph of Uriah and Littimer, and perhaps even believing in the escape of the Micawbers and the remains of Mr. Peggotty's little band into some other world, less critically real, where they can try life over again. Indeed, we must accept this last, however unsatisfactory it may be. We must accept it from David, at any rate, for whom it is simply true; it is only Dickens with whom we may quarrel.

Yet our quarrel with Dickens can only be a minor one. He has achieved in this novel perhaps the climax of his art, and from it will come both the problems and the successes of the last six novels. Here, momentarily, the little pocket of love has transcended itself and achieved a reputable dignity by becoming responsible in and to the world. Reality has claimed almost all of the characters, Traddles and David in a particularly high and full sense, and two significant new "families" are established in the end of the novel.

To make a new "family" is to fit all the people who began the novel in a state of symbolic orphanage into new homes. Traddles does this by accommodating the numerous Misses Crewler after their mother's death, and he will try, as a judge, to accommodate the world. David organizes the various characters out of his past and houses them as his family—Miss Betsey, Mr. Dick, Peggotty, and his wife, Agnes. As a novelist David is more ambitious and, as we can tell from our experience as readers, quite successful. He so orders his "Experience" as to make the world more comprehensible and thus something more than tolerable. Mr. Dick no longer complains, and even the villains—at least two of them, Littimer and Heep—are accommodated. This large family of people, the inhabitants of the world of the novel, all take David's name; they live in and as members of *David Copperfield*.

In a way, David as a novelist is Dickens's wish fulfillment of his own personal and artistic ambitions. At the same time that the novel continues Dickens's romantic attack on the lovelessness of man, on man's inhumanity to man, it also accepts, with neither distortion nor exclusion, the world as it is. It tests the mythic worlds of Eden and Noah's Ark as retreats, finds them inadequate and vulnerable, and opts for hard work and clear sight in the real world instead. That it does this in the name of a novelist who has a "power of doing good," whose audience reads his works "with delight, with entertainment, with instruction" marks the seriousness of the novel's claim for itself. In requiring of its hero a charitable comprehension of the world, *David Copperfield* dramatizes the function of the artist as lover, and teaches Dickens how to remake the world. Mythically, the novel dramatizes the role of the artist as Noah, and teaches Dickens what his myth of recreation must be in the novels which come after it.

4

BLEAK HOUSE AND LITTLE DORRIT

1

IN *Bleak House* AND *Little Dorrit* DICKENS TAKES ON "THE system": society as it is organized by civilization, by the state. The Court of Chancery in *Bleak House* and the Circumlocution Office in *Little Dorrit* are the institutions which run—or, rather, don't run—the nation; the parasite lawyers of *Bleak House* and the Barnacle collection in *Little Dorrit* are all specialists in "How Not to Do It." The business of both Chancery and the Circumlocution Office is the perpetuation of the system, and thus it is the whole system, the law which governs it and the administration which organizes it, that Dickens attacks. The task he sets for himself in these novels is the exposure of the system. In the execution of this task, however, he transcends it, and what begins as reformist criticism becomes radical idealism.

The image that Dickens connects with the conservationist activity of those who defend the system—lawyers, bureaucrats— is that of surface. To maintain a surface, a glaze, a veneer of stability and decorous order is the aim of systematized life. As Conversation Kenge, one of the lawyers in *Bleak House*, speaks of England's "great system," he is described as "gently moving his right hand as if it were a silver trowel, with which to spread the cement of his words on the structure of the system, and consolidate it for a thousand ages" (BH, p. 844). Earlier Dickens speaks of "ladies and gentlemen . . . very elegant, who have agreed to put a smooth glaze on the world, and to keep down all its realities. For whom everything must be languid and pretty. Who have found the perpetual stoppage. . . . Who are not to be disturbed by ideas" (BH, p. 160). Like Mr. Podsnap in *Our Mutual Friend*, they don't want to know anything unpleasant; like Mr. Veneering, they are happy admiring the reflections of themselves in the highly polished surface of class; like Mrs. General, "that eminent varnisher" (LD, p. 476), they are concerned with "the formation of a surface" which will enable any "truly refined mind . . . to be ignorant of the existence of anything that is not perfectly proper, placid, and pleasant" (LD, p. 477). For these people, "even the Fine Arts, attending in powder and walking backward like the Lord Chancellor, must . . . be particularly careful not to be in earnest, or to receive any impressions from the moving age" (BH, p. 160).

But art cannot accept this role of service to the system, and thus for those committed to the status quo, art must always seem subversive. As Hillis Miller has argued, time is the basic dimension of all fiction.[1] Life in time means change and being involves becoming. Thus Dickens's heroes are always changing, becoming; for the most part they are young men growing up. But metaphysically, change is the mark of finite imperfection as well as becoming, and in addition to change or growth in characters, there is a larger, general change that one must be aware of in Dickens's novels. For Dickens the whole world is in a state of flux. His critical vision sees this change as the need for social, political, and even moral reform, the movement of human society

---

1. J. Hillis Miller, *The Form of Victorian Fiction* (Notre Dame, Indiana, 1968), p. 6.

toward a more perfect order. Fearing such change the stalwarts of the status quo, like Sir Leicester Dedlock, wonder gravely "to what the present age is tending" (BH, p. 160).

A number of critics have focused their attention on people like the Dedlocks, whom Dickens criticizes and caricatures, and on the corrupt world of the status quo to which they cling. It seems to me that this emphasis is wrong. Reading just Dickens's "criticism" is like reading just his plots. Those critics who have marveled at the plot of *Bleak House* typically have failed to read what the plot means. For example: all the mystery of the novel is imaged as keeping secrets and collecting information—Tulkinghorn, Mr. Krook, Chancery itself, and Lady Dedlock are the most important keepers and collectors—and these activities are equated with "the perpetual stoppage" and the glazing of the surface. Dickens's response to the proponents of stoppage is violence: murder for Tulkinghorn, spontaneous combustion for Mr. Krook, disintegration into coats and bags of paper—diarrhea? —for the great suit in Chancery, and death for Lady Dedlock. The mystery of Tulkinghorn's murder is only half a mystery; that Hortense kills him is important for us because she is metaphorically as well as literally Lady Dedlock's double, and she acts for Lady Dedlock just as in *Great Expectations* Orlick acts for Pip in attacking Mrs. Joe. The plot of *Bleak House* contains other mysteries, too; but what we are led to through these mysteries is not just their solution. More importantly, we are led through these plot devices to Dickens's criticism, and through that to the meaning of the novel. Dickens's answer to the "stoppage" and the "glaze" and the "system" is not just the violence of murder and spontaneous combustion, it is the exposure of all the secrets hidden under the surface of the system, the exposure of the failure of the system to make or keep order.

If we look at the sequence of events in *Bleak House* more as form and meaning than as plot, the center of the novel becomes the death of Little Jo. Surface and stoppage and status quo say,

8 5

through Mr. Bucket's fat finger, that Jo must "move on." He must not be seen. And when he dies, no one must know, for no one should care. Dickens's response to this event is much like his response to Chancery, which he wants to blow up; and when Jo dies, he sets the charge under the system and blows up the surface that reflects the "languid and pretty," to show us all this world's realities:

> Dead, your Majesty. Dead, my lords and gentlemen. Dead, Right Reverends and Wrong Reverends of every order. Dead, men and women, born with heavenly compassion in your hearts. And dying thus around us every day. (BH, p. 649)

The rhetoric here is the same that Dickens uses when he blows up Mr. Krook, but the spontaneous combustion of Krook is symbolic, and its rhetorical significance for Dickens is more as a psychological release. The rhetoric with which he attacks society after the death of Jo has a more real and literal effect than that. This later explosion literally breaks the surface glaze; and the rest of the novel consists in part of Dickens's exposure of the ugly truths hidden beneath. This exposure of evil (it was called an "explosion" and "Vesuvius" in *David Copperfield*) is one of the functions of art for Dickens. For him the explosion is as paradoxical as the "big bang" of the creation of the universe, or the cataclysm of the Flood; and in this is the second function of art. We learn from the exposure of evil, and we create something new out of the catastrophe. True, though evil is exposed, the more perfect order never comes in this or any other Dickens novel; but perfection achieved is no more the point than is the violence of his attack upon corruption. The greatness of Dickens's vision here is in the hope he can find for a better order—a hope that enables us to go on living.

When Little Jo is dying, Allan Woodcourt tries praying with him; but Jo "never knowd nothink," and has never prayed before (BH, p. 648). The most powerful irony of Jo's death comes as he finally begins to pray under Allan's tutelage. "OUR FATHER," says Allan; and Jo repeats, "Our Father—yes, that's wery good, sir" (BH, p. 649). But Jo is not praying to God, whom he doesn't know. An orphan, Jo is "praying" to the first "father" he has ever known *in this world*—to the good man of the novel, Allan Woodcourt. As Jo is dying and his sight fails, he asks if there is "any light a-comin?" (BH, p. 699)—meaning natural, not supernatural light. And in this novel of Dickens's maturity, the light that comes, as Allan promises Jo it will, is not the light of heaven, but the light that discovers the evils of this world. As Richard Carstone dies, at the end of the novel, he has "a light in his eyes" as he speaks of having lived "a trouble dream" (BH, p. 870). As he dies, proposing to "begin the world," Dickens laments, bitterly and ironically, that Richard is beginning too late and must therefore begin "not this world, O not this! The world that sets this right" (BH, p. 871). It is perhaps a dark realism that says this world will never set itself right completely; but it is a noble vision that insists on the efficacy of enlightening goodness that can begin, in however small a way, to do the work of right and change. And though Richard dies to leave this world, there is a new beginning in it, as Esther and Allan move to the new "Bleak House" on what Mr. Jarndyce calls "the brightest day in all my life" (BH, p. 858).

If we look at Dickens's mythic vision, again, rather than his immediately critical vision, we can perhaps better understand the complex way he uses change. In his mythic vision, the change, the becoming, is the crisis of creation. The question for Dickens, over and over and over again, is whether in its imperfect state this world of ours is evolving backward or forward, toward or away from perfection. Thus the times—the mythic times—in which the novels are set are those of Genesis: of the Creation, Eden, the Deluge. The question Dickens is asking through the use of this mythology is, can our world evolve into order, or must there be a catastrophe, after which we can make a new beginning? Part of the answer to this question is submerged in the symbols of Krook's spontaneous combustion in *Bleak House*, the disintegration of the Clennam house in *Little Dorrit*, and the removal of the mounds in *Our Mutual Friend*. And perhaps it is stated in Stephen Blackpool's words in *Hard Times*: things won't get better, there will be no love "till th' Sun turns t' ice. . . . till God's work is onmade" (HT, p. 151). But this is only part of the answer. The other part is in the growth of certain characters in this time of crisis and the association of their growth with the resolution of the mythic, metaphysical order.

The question of where the world is going is more central and more critical in *Bleak House* and *Little Dorrit* than in any other of Dickens's novels. This may be so because in these two novels he is challenging institutional, civilized order directly: Chancery is a real, literal institution, and in *Bleak House* it stands for the whole idea of society under law; the Circumlocution Office is a metaphorical institution—which both Dickens and his characters treat as real—standing for civilized government. The complex plots of both novels center on these symbols, and everything is threaded through them. Neither Chancery nor the Circumlocution Office is destroyed in the end—Dickens was too much a realist for that—but there is a new beginning in the end of each. Esther and Allan Woodcourt are established in the new "Bleak House," to work in the world and do good; Amy and Arthur Clennam go "down" into the world, "into a modest life of usefulness and happiness" (LD, p. 826). These new beginnings are not dramatized; we are told of them in the traditional wrapping-up of the story. They are satisfactory, nevertheless. That Dickens wins these new beginnings within the world of chaos is one of the triumphs of his art; and they are won through the successful resolution of plot or story with myth and vision. The myth through which he elaborates and tests his vision settles at last back onto the particular time from which it was generated, and in the end we all know—Dickens, his heroes, us—that we cannot recreate Eden; that we cannot escape and be saved on Noah's Ark; that the only way that Chancery and the Circumlocution Office can ever be overcome is through the loving effect of works and lives like those of Esther and Allan, Amy and Arthur. All of this knowledge, the darkness and the hope, is important.

Bleak House opens in an intensely present time—the participial construction makes for this—which is also the third day of the Creation:

> London. . . . As much mud in the streets, as if the waters had but newly retired from the face of the earth, and it would not be wonderful to meet a Megalosaurus, forty feet long or so, waddling like an elephantine lizard up Holborn Hill. (BH, p. 1)

This is the uncreated universe. There are "Dogs, undistinguishable in the mire. Horses, scarcely better." Everything, including man's concrete and stone attempts at order, everything is slipping back into the aboriginal chaos: "Foot passengers . . . losing their foothold at street-corners, where tens of thousands of other foot passengers have been slipping and sliding since the day broke" (BH, p. 1). And yet, for all that this is such an early time in history, Jarndyce and Jarndyce is already old, and makes a whole world history of outrage and futility unto itself:

> Jarndyce and Jarndyce drones on. . . . Innumerable children have been born into the cause: innumerable young people have married into it; innumerable old people have died out of it. Scores of persons have deliriously found themselves made parties in Jarndyce and Jarndyce, without knowing how or why; whole families have inherited legendary hatreds with the suit. (BH, p. 4)

Jarndyce and Jarndyce is in Chancery, of course; and Chancery sits "in the midst of the mud and the heart of the fog" (BH, p. 5) that rises from the mire on this third day. Chancery is the law, the alleged means of ordering the chaos, of righting wrong, of governing, of administering justice; but Chancery has no light, no hope. Indeed, Chancery governs the chaos by preserving it as it is; and though the chaos is universal—"the Court of Chancery . . . has its decaying houses and blighted lands in every shire" (BH, p. 203)—Chancery still defends things as they are. Chancery is "the system." Though Dickens would like to destroy it, the whole to be "burnt away in a great funeral pyre" (BH, p. 7) or, as Mr. Boythorne proposes, "the infernal cauldron" to be "blown to atoms with ten thousand hundredweight of gunpowder" (BH, p. 118), he knows that reform cannot come so easily. Relief will come on "the Day of Judgment" (BH, pp. 33 ff.), no sooner. From the beginning to the end there is chaos, it seems.

Chesney Wold, the fashionable home of the status quo, is much like Chancery: "It is not so unlike the Court of Chancery, but that we may pass from one scene to the other, as the crow flies" (BH, p. 8). What we see, flying thus, is that history is at a similar point in time in the world of fashion to what it was in the London of Chancery:

> The waters are out in Lincolnshire. An arch of the bridge in the park has been sapped and sopped away. The adjacent low-lying ground, for half a mile in breadth, is a stagnant river, with melancholy trees for islands in it, and a surface punctured all over, all day long, with falling rain. (BH, p. 8)

But it is no longer the third day of Creation; rather, rain has been falling at Chesney Wold "for many a day and night" (BH, p. 8), and the waters are almost at the flood. Soon "the country [will be] shipwrecked, lost, and gone to pieces" (BH, p. 161), for the country will not take warning "as the old world did in the days before the flood" (BH, p. 562). Sir Leicester uses the same metaphor, seeing his world begin to collapse: "the floodgates of society are burst open, and the waters have—a—obliterated the landmarks of the framework of the cohesion by which things are held together" (BH, pp. 570-71).[2] The time is one of crisis:

2. That the collapse is the collapse of the class society is clearer from Sir

the Deluge is upon us. And Peepy Jellyby, an innocent, unfortunate son of institutionalized charity, one of those millions lost in the chaos, clings to his toy Ark and carries Noah about with him, hoping to be saved, waiting for a savior (BH, pp. 423-24).

These scenes are not connected in this way in the plot of *Bleak House*, of course, nor are they the actual story Dickens is telling. They are metaphors from that story, however, and evidences of the myth he is using. What Dickens's imagination blends into his story is the mythology of Genesis. Thus when "the floodgates of society" are opened, and the political ship of state foundered, wrecked, and lost, and when young Peepy stands with his toy Noah (from the Ark which Esther gave him) waiting to be saved, a savior can be expected. He comes in the person of Allan Woodcourt, the hero of a shipwreck:

> "Well, my dear [Miss Flite reports], there has been a terrible shipwreck. . . . An awful scene. Death in all shapes. Hundreds of dead and dying. Fire, storm, and darkness. Numbers of the drowning thrown upon a rock. There, and through it all, my dear physician was a hero. Calm and brave, through everything. Saved many lives . . . took the lead, showed them what to do, governed them, tended the sick, buried the dead, and brought the poor survivors safely off at last." (BH, p. 500)

To explain what Allan's mythic heroism means in the more particular context of the story of *Bleak House* and to find out how story and myth are resolved together, it is necessary to examine closely several of the arguments and focuses of that story. Mythically, the novel describes Dickens's vision of universal chaos; dramatically, *Bleak House* is a coherent, radical assault on the society that is organized, civilized, according to the rule of

---

Leicester's earlier use of the same image. Dickens reports the "swift progress of the Dedlock mind" as it envisions "the whole framework of society, . . . receiving tremendous cracks in consequence of people . . . getting out of the station unto which they are called . . . and so obliterating the landmarks, and opening the floodgates, and all the rest of it" (BH, p. 397).

law. But motivating both the myth and the story is Dickens's idealism, and thus the end of the novel is not pessimistic or desperate but full of hope. His early solution to the problems of this mad world was a retreat to Eden. Now he knows that there is no such place, though he still needs it. Similarly, his social criticism becomes both harsher and more general during the course of his career, at the same time that his philosophical conception of love grows away from sentimentalism and toward rational idealism. In both cases, his awareness of the chaos and his sense of the need for order seem to develop together, almost as functions of each other.[3]

Dickens organizes the story of *Bleak House* around four characters, all of them involved with Chancery: Esther Summerson, John Jarndyce, Little Jo, and Mr. Krook. Esther, a ward of the court, narrates almost half the novel. Her marriage to Allan Woodcourt is the affirmative climax of Dickens's ideal vision, though her often saccharine goodness is a bothersome indication of the still sentimental and romantic side of that vision. Esther is in part another version of that "principle of Good" or "principle of Love," along with Oliver and David. Significantly for a first person narrator, one of her many names is "Dame Trot" which is surely a borrowing from "Trotwood" Copperfield. John Jarndyce, her guardian, is both a director of the life of the novel and a spokesman for Dickens himself. Jarndyce sees society as it is represented by its institutions, by Chancery primarily, by the legal institution and by its alleged order, as evil; and in serving as the moral director of Esther's and Allan's lives, the would-be counselor of Richard Carstone, and the protector of Ada Clare, he becomes Dickens's sceptical spokesman against all institutions and against the formulation of society upon an institutional basis. The life and death of Jo are exemplary of the effect of the

---

3. Mr. Jellyby, for example, comes alive but once in the novel. Esther reports that he "became interested" when he saw that she and Caddy "were attempting to establish some order among all the waste and ruin" (BH, p. 420).

general corruption of institutional civilization on a particular creature, and the destruction of Krook demonstrates the awful extreme of Dickens's most radical solution to this corruption.

Jo's role in the novel, for Dickens, is that of the innocent destroyed by society and its institutions. Jo is a crossing sweeper; and as such he devotes his life, symbolically, to the impossible task of sweeping the dust and mud of this earth off the dirt and cobblestone streets of the world. He is the child of bondage, living in Tom-All-Alone's, which is "in Chancery" as a part of the great suit of Jarndyce and Jarndyce; and in the end, his death is purchased, literally, by the agent of the law, Mr. Bucket. Dickens's agony at Jo's death is that Jo has seen nothing good or beautiful on this earth; the first good thing he finds is in the father-prayer which Woodcourt begins to teach him as he dies. Jo stands as plaintiff, witness, and primary exhibit in the case of Man vs. Society; and the pitch of Dickens's passion is defined in the grand but monstrous rhetoric of the editorial remark with which he concludes Jo's death scene.

Jo is killed by the world which he cannot understand. Its order—the order of law, the order of religion, the order of work, the order of charity—has nothing to do with him. Society, however, supports Mr. Krook who feeds upon it, symbolically, mimicking the Lord Chancellor in his Rag and Bottle shop. As "brother" to the Lord Chancellor, Krook is a kind of safety valve for Dickens. Chancery represents the primary controlling institution of life in society, the institution of courts and laws. Krook stands in for Chancery and its Lord Chancellor symbolically; the identification is founded on his hoarding, anal greed for dust and debris of all kinds. At what seems to be a moment at which the truth of the artist's imagination is overcome by the pressures of his psychological needs, Dickens wipes Krook out of existence, making him the victim of "spontaneous combustion." The destruction of Krook is Dickens's radical but artificial symbolic judgment upon Chancery, and thus upon civilization. The attempt to organize the chaos into civilization on the basis of law is failing; Chancery "has its decaying houses and its blighted lands in every shire." The image is Dickens's usual one for the failure of social order: that which man has attempted to form and create by means of the law, the principle ordering agency of civilization, is returning whence it came, to chaos.[4] The universality of this failure is described in the pervasiveness of Chancery's blight: "every shire" is the metaphor here for the whole civilized world. As it is constituted, as it has been instituted, civilization is evil. What man has made out of the first mud is hell; and the warning given in relation to Chancery is like Dante's over the gates of hell: "Suffer any wrong that can be done you rather than come here."

The ambition of *Bleak House* is to destroy Chancery and to remake society on the new order of love rather than the law. Chancery stands for "the system"; and the system is corrupt, the idea of systematization corrupting. Gridley complains of this to Jarndyce: "The system! I am told, on all hands, it's the system. I mustn't look to individuals. It's the system. I mustn't go into Court, and say, 'My Lord, I beg to know this from you—is this right or wrong? . . .' My Lord knows nothing of it. He sits there, to administer the system" (BH, p. 215). Dickens's earnest wish for an end to Chancery is introduced at the end of the opening chapter of the novel, and repeated by Mr. Boythorn's desire to blow up that "infernal cauldron" of "records, rules, precedents" with "a mine below it on a busy day in term time" (BH, p. 118). But Dickens cannot destroy the old order literally—cannot overthrow "the system" in this way—and remain within the bounds of realism. So, instead, he destroys its disgusting symbolic equiv-

---

4. Richard sees his own disturbance (being in Chancery) in a variation of this same metaphor of architectural disorder: "If you were living in an unfinished house, liable to have the roof put on or taken off—to be from top to bottom pulled down or built up—tomorrow, next day, next week, next month, next year—you would find it hard to rest or settle. So do I" (BH, p. 524).

alent, Mr. Krook.[5] Sentimentally, Dickens eliminates Krook from
existence to satisfy his own urgent dreams for the ideal freedom
of the world. The assertion he makes of the moral—not aesthetic
—justness of Krook's destruction gives us a sure key to the intense psychological and philosophical argument which is imaged
and fictionalized in this novel:

> The Lord Chancellor of that Court, true to his title to his last act,
> has died the death of all Lord Chancellors in all Courts, and of all
> authorities in all places under all names soever, where false pretences
> are made, and where injustice is done. Call the death by any name
> your Highness will, attribute it to whom you will, or say it might have
> been prevented how you will, it is the same death eternally—inborn,
> inbred, engendered in the corrupted humours of the vicious body it-
> self, and that only—Spontaneous Combustion, and none other of all
> the deaths that can be died. (BH, pp. 455-56)

It is only a short step from this to the various dismissals of legal
justice, its agents, and its practices, through the later pages of the
novel. The law is the institutionalized agency of subversion, perversion, and destruction; and the man who would save himself
must avoid its insidious contamination. The only authority Dickens recognizes finally, is the law of love, and even that can be
destroyed by being institutionalized.

Dickens's philosophical position in *Bleak House* is close to that
of the classical anarchist-idealist, though certainly he could never
have realized or admitted this. He is opposed to all institutions,
no matter whether they are philanthropic, religious, economic,
political, educational, social, or legal. The revolution which Dickens wants to see take place is an absolute one, as extreme as that
occasioned by the Deluge. Working from this mythic and symbolic prophecy of change, Dickens particularizes his attack on

---

5. A connection of another kind might be argued between Dickens's obliter-
ation of Mr. Krook and the anarchists' attempt on the Greenwich Observatory in
The Secret Agent—both aimed at symbols of "the system."

the institution of law in the real world of the novel and its action. The law protects society; and in praising Inspector Bucket for being "faithful to his duty and perfectly right," Sir Leicester remarks that "it does not become us, who assist in making the laws to impede or interfere with those who carry them into execution. . . . or who vindicate their outraged majesty" (BH, pp. 718-19). The system is incestuously corrupt and can only be praised by people like Sir Leicester whom it protects, or Vholes, who feeds on its carrion flesh, or Kenge, another of its employees:

> "We are a prosperous community, Mr. Jarndyce, a very prosperous community [said Mr. Kenge]. We are a very great country, Mr. Jarndyce, we are a very great country. This is a great system, Mr. Jarndyce, and would you wish a great country to have a little system? Now, really! really!" He said this at the stair-head, gently moving his right hand as if it were a silver trowel, with which to spread the cement of his words on the structure of the system, and consolidate it for a thousand ages. (BH, p. 844)

One way to recognize good people in Dickens's world is by their opposition to the system. Such goodness, however, is often naïveté and innocence as well. In a speech that echoes the words of another and earlier innocent, Mr. Pickwick, Mr. George denies the justness of such justice as is practiced and meted out in courts of law:

> "I must come off clear and full or not at all. Therefore, when I hear stated against me what is true, I say it's true; and when they tell me, 'whatever you say will be used,' I tell them I don't mind that; I mean it to be used. If they can't make me innocent out of the whole truth, they are not likely to do it out of anything less, or anything else. And if they are, it's worth nothing to me." (BH, pp. 706-07)

The voice is the voice of naïveté, but it is also the voice of essential goodness and morality. Courts of law are not concerned with justice and truth, according to Dickens.

96

John Jarndyce knows this—knows it more firmly, more surely
than Mr. George knows it. Jarndyce has few illusions. Like Mr.
Pickwick, this benevolent man has retired generally from active
participation in a corrupt and corrupting world. But Jarndyce's
retirement is not just retreat—like Pickwick's—and the modifi-
cation is important. Jarndyce is sceptical about the prospect that
any real good may come from the world as it is. He asks Kenge,
"Did you ever know English law, or equity either, plain and to the
purpose?" (BH, p. 842) and he complains to Esther of the fruit
of judicial practice:

> "Ah, Dame Trot, Dame Trot! . . . what shall we find reasonable
> in Jarndyce and Jarndyce! Unreason and injustice at the heart and at
> the bottom, unreason and injustice from beginning to end—if it ever
> has an end." (BH, p. 814)

This scepticism, however, is but a part of Jarndyce's total view of
the world, and like Dickens he matches his criticism with hope.
Though he has removed himself from the world at large, he is
engaged in preparing others to meet it. This is the function of
his orphanage and school at Bleak House. Jarndyce believes in
the possibility of change, through the agency of individual moral
action. His best pupil is Esther, and she learns to love the novel's
good young man.

Esther has known all along that the best ambition she can have
in life is "to do good to some one, and win some love to [her]self
if [she] could" (BH, p. 495). In answer to Pardigglean and Jel-
lybyan charity, Esther writes: "I thought it best to be as useful as
I could, to those immediately about; and to try to let that circle
of duty gradually and naturally expand itself" (BH, p. 104).
And Allan, the "noble," "generous" hero of the shipwreck who
is "so truly good and brave" (BH, pp. 500-501), "so useful and
brave" (BH, p. 623), is the doctor who aids and attends Miss
Flite and Caddy in their illnesses, befriends and ministers to Jo,
and tries to save Richard. Allan is not a particularly well-drawn

character in the novel, but it is obvious what he represents for Dickens.[6] He deserves by his goodness and his love for others "to be made rich," and that goodness, like David's art, is a power which makes him "so useful ... [that] there might be many who could ill spare him" (BH, p. 686). He is finally a man dedicated to a reality of moral action and to the idea of improvement. As Jarndyce tells Esther, Allan is "a man whose hopes and aims may sometimes lie ... above the ordinary level," and who is committed, whatever the situation may be, to "a way of usefulness and good service" (BH, p. 816). The firmness and stability of Allan's promises—and Dickens appreciates this—is expressed by Jarndyce's conclusion that "All generous spirits are ambitious, I suppose; but the ambition that calmly trusts itself to such a road, instead of spasmodically trying to fly over it, is of the kind I care for. It is Woodcourt's kind" (BH, p. 816). Esther's guardian then gives her to Allan, with his and Dickens's blessings. And having done this, Jarndyce can "revert to [his] bachelor habits" (BH, p. 859), with the knowledge that they will love and act together in the world.

Until Esther and Allan can be united, however, Jarndyce's hope is hard for him to assert and hard for us to find. The system demoralizes him because it is too large for him to correct or control; and the suit frustrates him, an example of "unreason and injustice from beginning to end—if it ever has an end." But Jarndyce and Jarndyce does have an end, finally—is dissolved into costs and "great bundles of paper" (BH, p. 865). Miss Flite frees her birds—which must mean something like "the Day of Judgment" that she so often refers to is at hand—and a new world is begun. "Beginning the World", the title of chapter 65, refers directly to Richard's pathetic last resolution; it also refers, however, to the mythic time structure of the novel, which began "in

---

6. As hero of the shipwreck, Allan is Noah, of course. Esther's other young suitor is Mr. Guppy, who is but a small fish!

the beginning," when the world was as deep in fog and mud "as if the waters had but newly retired from the face of the earth," and now ends with a new beginning. But Dickens has not overthrown the corrupt society of institutions and their injustices, of course; his imagination is still and essentially grounded in the realism of experience. Thus, although the mythic time seems again at the end of the novel to be that of the Deluge, the world poor Richard "will begin" is "Not this world, O not this!" but "The world that sets this right" (BH, pp. 870-71). Yet Dickens has closed Chesney Wold (BH, pp. 875-76) and the East wind has ceased to blow (BH, p. 879). And although the final chapter is marred aesthetically by the sentimental excesses of Esther's romantic piety, still it closes with the dramatic affirmation of love as moral action. What was but a principle—and Esther is called a "pattern young lady" (BH, p. 852)—is embodied now in the real married union of Esther and Allan. This new world must surely be a better place, in its time, than was the one we have just lived through.

2

To speak of better places and better times to come in Dickens's later novels is either to speak sentimentally (or ironically) of another life beyond this world, or to speak of a very hard, small hope for a future to be made better here by earnest work. Heaven is irrelevant—despite what Sydney Carton says at the end of *A Tale of Two Cities*—and miraculously achieved or discovered utopias are an impossibility. This is perhaps most clear in the conclusion to *Little Dorrit*, in which Amy and Arthur Clennam are married and set out on a new generation of life beyond the novel. After the wedding,

> They paused for a moment on the steps of the portico, looking at the fresh perspective of the street in the autumn morning sun's bright rays, and then went down.

99

Went down into a modest life of usefulness and happiness. Went down to give a mother's care, in the fulness of time, to Fanny's neglected children no less than to their own. . . . Went down to give a tender nurse and friend to Tip for some few years. . . . They went quietly down into the roaring streets, inseparable and blessed; and as they passed along in sunshine and shade, the noisy and the eager, and the arrogant and the froward and the vain, fretted and chafed, and made their usual uproar. (LD, p. 826)

It would be wonderful if they could go down into a happier, more perfect world, but there is no such world. Dickens's poetry makes this clear: the "fresh perspective of the street" is qualified by the sun's being an "autumn" sun; and they go "down" into the world to find both their happiness and their usefulness. Some fifteen months after writing these words about Amy's and Arthur's future, Dickens wrote much more explicitly to Wilkie Collins on the same subject:

Everything that happens . . . shows beyond mistake that you can't shut out the world; that you are in it, to be of it; that you get into a false position the moment you try to sever yourself from it; and that you must mingle with it, and make the best of it, and make the best of yourself into the bargain.[7]

The world of Little Dorrit is insistently postlapsarian, and Dickens is unwilling to fabricate it otherwise, except in a small, comic way at "Happy Cottage," the "counterfeit cottage," the "wonderful deception" Mrs. Plornish creates behind the back wall of her shop (LD, p. 574). Elsewhere, the consistent and repeated "pattern of the universe" (LD, p. 234) is chaos, a "maze" (LD, pp. 234, 432), a "labyrinth" (LD, pp. 221, 324, 408, 464, 556, 820), a "wilderness" (LD, pp. 99, 144, 161, 324, 542, 637). There is no Eden; rather, the world is a "labyrinth trodden by the sons of Adam" (LD, p. 556). Cain appears as a wanderer

---

7. Dickens to Collins, 6 September 1858; Dickens finished writing *Little Dorrit* in the spring of 1857.

(LD, p. 124), and there is a reminder of "Abel's murder" (LD, p. 267). There are a number of reminders that our inheritance is from Adam. Mrs. Clennam insists that "all the children of Adam" have "offenses to expiate" (LD, p. 356), and Mrs. Merdle laments hypocritically that we don't live "in a more primitive state" (LD, pp. 242, 391). Early in the novel Dickens remarks on the pervasiveness of mud on a rainy day as mud which "splashed all the sons and daughters of Adam" (LD, p. 30). What this last reference seems to question is the success of the creation itself; and later Dickens suggests that, given the way things are, it might have been better if "the earth . . . never [had] been made, or, if made in a rash mistake. . . . [had] remained blank mud" (LD, p. 406). Of course the mud itself is corrupt in this fallen world. It is turned, as various Freudian critics have pointed out, to money—and money's pervasive name is Merdle: "wherever he went, he saw, or heard, or touched, the celebrated name of Merdle" (LD, p. 585); "Merdle, Merdle, Merdle. Always Merdle" (LD, p. 581). Mr. Dorrit asserts that "The name of Merdle is the name of the age" (LD, p. 484); and to make certain of the linguistic connection, Dickens even has the name pronounced once as "*Mair*dale" (LD, p. 614).

In a world so corrupted that what should be Eden is offal, there is hardly room for idealism. Daniel Doyce is Dickens's only idealist in the novel, and his dreams can only be fulfilled outside England which is, in effect, beyond this world. Little Dorrit is not an idealist, but is an ideal creature. She is like an "angel" to Clennam (LD, pp. 756, 816), and in order to keep her such, both Dickens and his hero have to treat her like a child. As the hero, Clennam must fulfill himself with or complete himself in both of these "unspoilt" and "simple" (LD, p. 309) people. The choice of initials, as so often in Dickens, reinforces both of these connections: completion means Clennam/Doyce as well as Clennam/Dorrit.

Daniel's invention—"The thing is as true as it ever was" (LD,

p. 190) is the best description of it that we are given—is useless in England because it is both commonsensical and idealistic. We are never told what it is; only that it is a thing made. I would speculate that the great invention is or perhaps, means, love; that what this romantic engineer makes but cannot market in England is ideal form. In a novel which makes the Circumlocution Office an acceptable reality, and which invents a "certain barbaric Power" (the inversion is Blakean rather than Rousseauistic) to utilize Doyce's invention, it is conceivable to think of love as that invention, as a "thing" that is "as true as it ever was." To Doyce himself, we are told, the invention seems "as if the Divine artificer had made it, and he had happened to find it" (LD, p. 516), suggesting even more the mythic curiosity of this creation. Earlier, when Henry Gowan remarks on Doyce's idealism, he uses language pertinent to the Genesis myth to describe him as someone who belongs to another world: "So fresh, so green, trusts in such wonderful things" (LD, p. 309). Conceivably, such an innocent might invent or discover love. The invention is never actually used in the novel. The closest it comes is in chapter 8 of Book the Second, which opens with a discussion of the invention and Arthur's work for it against the Circumlocution Office. The chapter then turns, curiously, to his thoughts about Little Dorrit and about whom she will marry. It is this kind of thought, the thought of Amy as other than a child, that Clennam must learn before he can really love her; and perhaps his work on the invention makes him start thinking this way.

At any rate, out of all the darkness and chaos of the novel comes love. Amy, the "angel," has always been love, or another "principle of Love"; at the end, however, she and Arthur are not love but loving, and even though the world hasn't changed, their change is significant enough in itself to make a satisfactory conclusion. When Arthur goes to the Marshalsea to congratulate Mr. Dorrit on his inheritance he also congratulates him "on the happy future" into which he can now carry Amy, whom he calls a "treasure . . . the best of all the riches you can have" (LD, p. 418). Amy uses the same metaphor at the end of the novel when she comes to visit Clennam in that prison to tell him she has no money, but is "rich" in his love (LD, p. 817). Merdle is dead, the money that has infected the novel has disappeared, and the truly valuable thing, love, is found.

At the end of novels like *David Copperfield, Bleak House, Little Dorrit, Great Expectations,* and *Our Mutual Friend* we experience a kind of catharsis which is not a product of plot and character situation, but comes to us rather from the mythic dimension of the novel. This mythic experience is something like Oliver Twist's fear of being hanged and his release from that fear: a psychological experience which we are given to feel, to sense, through the imagery of hanging that pervades the novel. The experience is much like the experience of tragedy, though it is wrong, it seems to me, to call any of these later novels tragedies. In most of the novels after *David Copperfield* there is an important dimension of communication between the reader and the author which is not available to the consciousness of the characters.[8] This dimension is the mythic dimension which impresses upon us a terribly intense awareness of the universal chaos of the world—an awareness which transcends that of any of the characters, even though they live in the midst of it all. The resolutions of these novels involve our release from this overriding sense of chaos. The crisis of history seems suddenly to pass, and we return from our abnormal perspective to see good friends of strong character go out to work in the world for change.

Thus for all that Dickens's mythic vision originates in chaos, it is not finally cataclysmic. To be sure, he is tempted at times toward a Nietzschean dream of destroying everything in hopes

---

8. An exception may be Esther Summerson as she grows through the novel to see things more and more as Dickens sees them, and writes accordingly; the same is not true of *David Copperfield* or *Great Expectations*, since there the narrators are different from themselves as characters.

that something better will take its place. But he never gives in to that temptation, else he would have blown up Chancery, rather than Mr. Krook, and destroyed the Circumlocution Office instead of the Clennam house. In terms of his mythic vision, the destruction of the world is always compromised by Noah and the Ark. This figure is finally the most important in his whole mythology, for without it there is no hope for us: without it, when the waters recede it is the third day of the Creation again, and we have all been destroyed.

Little Dorrit offers us a more coherent formulation of Dickens's mythology and the resolution it helps to make than any of his other works. I have already discussed the collection of Genesis references to Adam and the primitive world, which make a pattern of postlapsarian imagery insisting on the general corruption of this place and denying the possibility of a retreat to Eden. As usual in Dickens, all of Genesis makes one myth so that the Creation, Eden and the Fall, the Flood, and even Babel and its catastrophe are united. "Babel" appears by name in *Little Dorrit* early (LD, p. 1); its effect, however, appears throughout, in the inability of people to communicate with each other. Mr. Dorrit's speech is always "fragmentary" (LD, p. 477); Mrs. General can say only "Papa, potatoes, poultry, prunes, and prism" (LD, pp. 876 ff.); Flora is cursed with an almost unbelievable "loquacity" (LD, p. 282) of "scattered words" (LD, p. 213); Mr. Plornish is always "a little obscure" (LD, p. 280); Mr. Rugg is "a man of many words" (LD, p. 299), which means, of course, many more than he needs; Mrs. Plornish is a pidgin "linguist" (LD, p. 732) in her role as interpreter for Cavalletto; Mr. Meagles will not attempt foreign languages; Mr. F.'s Aunt speaks in mad non sequiturs; and Mr. Nandy uses words like children use bubble gum, to keep his mouth busy.[9] And the central symbol of

9. This pattern of noncommunication in Dickens was first pointed out to me by Robert J. Heaman; see his essay on *Little Dorrit* in "Love and Adversity in the Novels of Charles Dickens," cited above.

the novel is an image of the tower of Babel: the Circumlocution Office.

The most important failure of communication is that which keeps Arthur and Amy from saying they love each other. Blandois says to Arthur, "Words, sir, never influence the course of the cards, or the course of the dice" (LD, p. 745); whether or not he is right about words and gaming, the point is that words—communications—are important and influential in life. Our inability to communicate with each other is one of the signs of our corruption. In this world of Babel, of chaos, there are silent people like Arthur and Amy—and Arthur's rival and double, young John Chivery, who cannot speak his love to Amy, but goes about composing wonderful epitaphs for himself in his head; and there are talkative people, like Flora and Mr. Nandy and all the parliamentary Barnacles whose many words say nothing. In the end of the novel, when Arthur and Amy have overcome their fears of speaking and of loving they are changed. But the rest of the world remains generally the same, and in its last characterization it is represented as still a "noisy" world of "roaring streets," where "the arrogant and the froward and the vain, fretted and chafed, and made their usual uproar" (LD, p. 826). It is clear: Arthur and Amy will have to learn to survive in the world of Babel.

The myth of the Flood is like the Babel myth in *Little Dorrit*. Only once is there a specific reference to the Ark, in the opening of Book the Second. There, when the Dorrits rest in the Alps at "the convent of the Great Saint Bernard," night comes "up the mountain like a rising water," and it seems "as if [the convent] were another Ark, and floated on the shadowy waves" (LD, p. 432). In this convent or Ark there is a smell "like the smell of a menagerie of wild animals" (LD, pp. 433-34). These references would have no special significance and might seem but reflex uses of the myth were it not that the novel is permeated with an imagery of water travel, nautical expressions, and metaphors of the sea.[10] When Dickens refers to Lord Decimus Tite Barnacle as "the Pilot of the ship" (LD, p. 405) he is using the common ship-of-state metaphor, extended with a suggestion that "the ship" can be kept "above water" only "by dint of hard pumping" on the part of the crew (LD, p. 405). Henry Gowan has earlier used the metaphor in the same way, remarking that "the Circumlocution Office may ultimately shipwreck everybody and everything" (LD, p. 310). When Mr. Merdle gives his special dinner to launch young Sparkler's political career, arrivals at the house are referred to as "ships" sailing in to dinner, as "vessels coming into port" (LD, p. 559). Bar is said to speak in a "legal current of speech" this evening, and the Barnacles, who cling to the ship nominally, are now called fishermen (LD, p. 561). Sparkler launched, he is said to have "stuck to his colours . . . a perfect Nelson in respect to nailing them to the mast" (LD, p. 805). Earlier, Sparkler's relation to Fanny Dorrit has been described as that of "a boat . . . when it is towed by a steam-ship" (LD, p. 593).

While such people as the Barnacles, Mr. Merdle, and young Sparkler are running the ship of state—and they run it so ruthlessly that Mr. Meagles is "hove down" by their wash (LD, p. 407)—there are other ships at sea as well, and the first references of their metaphors are various. The closest to the Barnacle ship-of-state metaphor is probably that of "the good ship Pancks" (LD, p. 539) whose hard-working busyness as a tugboat (LD, p. 297) gets things done. He is a "steam-vessel" (LD, p. 581), a "Steam-Tug" whose home is called a "Dock" (LD, pp. 797-99). When Pancks leaves work he is said to "cast off" (LD, p. 297); when he leaves a room he has "steamed out" (LD, p. 341) or

---

10. G. L. Brook, in *The Language of Dickens* (London, 1970), pp. 82-83, notes in passing the occasional appearance of nautical imagery as "class dialect" in both *Dombey and Son* and *Bleak House*. But even in *Dombey and Son* this kind of imagery does not become a substantive part of the novel, as it does in *Little Dorrit*.

"steamed away" (LD, p. 541). His constant busyness—he seems always to have "his utmost pressure of steam on" (LD, p. 799) —is invariably at someone else's business, someone else's work. He collects rents for the Patriarch, worries for everybody about Merdle and his money, and works out Mr. Dorrit's inheritance and release. The point may be that the world needs Panckses, people ready to do something when there is something to be done. Certainly a world full of Barnacles could be improved by a ration of Panckses.[11]

Other nautical personages in *Little Dorrit* are Cavalletto, who goes "with the stream of his fortunes" (LD, p. 302) and "make[s] head as well as he could" (LD, p. 303); Henry Gowan, whom Little Dorrit worries about as one of those "ships . . . in too shallow and rocky waters," whose "anchors had no hold, and they drifted anywhere" (LD, p. 495); and Fanny, whose "anchor" is Amy (LD, pp. 589, 593). Arthur is "liable to be drifted where any current may set" (LD, p. 20) in the beginning; and later, to demonstrate this point, it seems, he goes to "look at the shipping news . . . and even to exchange small socialities with mercantile Sea Captains" (LD, p. 340); later still, when he has begun to find out something about Blandois, his thoughts "rode at anchor by the haunting topic," and he seems like a prisoner in a prisonship, "a criminal chained in a stationary boat on a deep clear river" and tied to this thought (LD, p. 679).

All of these images raise the suggestion of danger. "Fear death by drowning" is the warning that comes through subliminally, mythically, in this vision of the Waste Land.[12] The darkness of Dickens's vision is in this warning, and however the plot of the

---

11. By a curious coincidence, a "Panku"—which is close enough to Pancks, especially when Cavaletto pronounces it "Panco"—is "a being personifying the primeval stuff from which heaven and earth were formed," in Oriental mythology (*Random House Dictionary* [New York, 1967], p. 1043).

12. It might not be too farfetched to suggest that the varnishers and surface polishers are really good shipbuilders, for their work is much like that needed to keep a boat from leaking.

novel is worked out, the darkness remains. Yet the darkness is not overwhelming. If it were, we would surely find the conclusions to the later novels unsatisfactory, for in each of them the story ends with the central characters fulfilled and, as Eugene Wrayburn says in *Our Mutual Friend*, ready to "turn to in earnest" (OMF, p. 812). Dickens resolves this disparity of the darkness and the happy ending by resolving myth with story. It is essentially a Noah resolution, for us: our sensible experience of the chaos is behind us, and now the good people are going out into the new world. Of course it is not a new world, because there is no new world, really, in the Noah myth. But there is a possibility for a successful and "useful" (LD, p. 826) life in the midst of the chaos, and that is our satisfaction.

This resolution is our catharsis. What is most convincing about *Bleak House, Little Dorrit,* and *Our Mutual Friend*—and perhaps about *Hard Times, A Tale of Two Cities,* and *Great Expectations* as well—is the darkness, the sensation that we feel of the corruption and chaos of our world. Our relief in these novels comes from the dedication of Dickens's heroes—those who have survived the trial of that chaos—to work in it. Esther and Allan work in the world, and the people "bless" them for it. The richness of their days is that Allan "has alleviated pain, and soothed some fellow-creature in the time of need" (BH, p. 879). Amy and Arthur go "down into a modest life of usefulness and happiness"—into a life which cares for other lives. These conclusions are not convincing dramatically: Woodcourt has not been a character in the novel, really, and we have hardly seen Clennam do anything particularly "useful"; Esther and Amy have been useful and good—too good, in fact, for their usefulness to be dramatically satisfactory. But it is not on a dramatic effect that the success of the resolution depends, and this is true of any nineteenth-century novel, from Jane Austen through Thomas Hardy. The resolution is the resolution of Dickens's vision of the world, as it is and as it could be, told through plot and character, embodied in the story. Our satisfaction comes from the fulfillment of the author's mythic generalizations within the real world we know and inhabit. We live much closer to the lives of Dickens's characters than we do to Noah's or Adam's mythic lives; yet when we submit ourselves to Dickens's art, we transcend our relative smallness and see our world through the enlarging metaphor of history. In the end, as we come back to ourselves, the myth is completed; there is a new generation. And with this new generation comes our new hope that love can be won from this chaos, that we can reorder the wilderness.

Novels like *Bleak House* and *Little Dorrit* are not in any way escapist, as most of Dickens's earlier novels were in their creation of pockets of love for their heroes to retreat to; and they are not pessimistic, as some of Dickens's recent critics have argued. Rather, they are optimistic, in the same way that tragedy is optimistic. Dickens manages this philosophic optimism by uniting the story with the myth, so that our larger mythic awareness of the troubles of this life can be salved by the example of a solution offered in the conclusion of the story, at the same time that our delight in this happy ending is tempered away from the unreality of the fairy tale and back to the universal reality on which the myth has insisted. The darkness of Dickens's vision is not overwhelming; rather, from within that darkness he finds the light. His common thesis that "right perception" is born out of "adversity" (LD, p. 720), applied usually to the particular situation of a character,[13] is a paradigm for the general resolution to these later novels.

What Dickens attacks in these novels is the desperate, unloving world we have made for ourselves in the name of society and civilization, the chaos we have made of our lives. What he champions is the possibility of reclaiming this world and reordering our lives, individually—one by one and two by two—through

---

13. See Heaman, "Love and Adversity in the Novels of Charles Dickens."

love. Dickens's imagination, passion, and compassion make the impressive strength of his attacks. His imagination, again, and the largeness of his faith, and the courage of his small, hard hope make what he projects for the future both believable and satisfying.

5

HARD TIMES AND A TALE OF TWO CITIES: TWO LATE FABLES

1

IT COULD BE ARGUED THAT CHRISTMAS IS AS SIGNIFICANT A myth for Dickens as Genesis, and indeed it is; but then in Christian terminology, both Noah and Adam are types of Christ, and Christ is "the new Adam." In Dickens's early novels Christmas is represented as a time for eating and drinking and being merry, not as a religious occasion. This Christmas is a time when men agree to pretend that both they and their world are innocent. In this early state Christmas is like the Eden which is a retreat from the world. But in Dickens's maturity—by the time of the later Christmas stories in the 1850's—Christmas takes on a very different symbolic character. In "What Christmas is as We Grow Older" (1851) he writes: "Nearer and closer to our hearts be the Christmas spirit, which is the spirit of active usefulness, perseverance, cheerful discharge of duty, kindness and forbearance!" (CS, p. 22). The portion of "The Holly-Tree Inn" (1855) which Dickens wrote ends:

> I began at the Holly-Tree, by idle accident, to associate the Christmas-time of year with human interest, and with some inquiry into, and

some care for, the lives of those by whom I find myself surrounded. I hope that I am none the worse for it, and that no one near me or afar off is the worse for it. (CS, p. 129)

And the thought expressed in "The Seven Poor Travellers" (1854) is "that Christmas comes but once a year,—which is unhappily too true, for when it begins to stay with us the whole year round we shall make this earth a very different place" (CS, p. 73).

These statements are arguments for action and change: not for political action or violent revolution, but personal moral action and that "metaphysical" change which will bring each of us to his "true self" (D&S, p. 73). However much Dickens's ideas may sound simplistic, abstracted from their dramatic context in this way, they are not so. He was not a pragmatic political philosopher, certainly; and he did not pretend to be so in his fiction. Rather, he attempts in his work to define in imaginative terms— in the terms of imaginative communication and understanding— the best future of the world, given things as they are now. Working in this context, he becomes a metaphysician of sorts; a metaphysician rather than a moralist. But *Hard Times*, a novel of the 1850's, can justly be called a moral fable. It is a Dickensian sermon containing a central moral exemplum, or dramatic parable, which is the story of the novel. Dickens's text for the sermon is, predictably, the "mad world." It is announced in the chapter appropriately entitled "The Key-Note":

Coketown . . . was a triumph of fact. . . . Let us strike the key-note, Coketown, before pursuing our tune.

It was a town of red brick, or of brick that would have been red if the smoke and ashes had allowed it; but as matters stood it was a town of unnatural red and black like the painted face of a savage. It was a town of machinery and tall chimneys, out of which interminable serpents of smoke trailed themselves for ever and ever, and never got uncoiled. It had a black canal in it, and a river that ran purple with ill-smelling dye, and vast piles of buildings full of windows where there was a rattling and a trembling all day long, and where the piston of the steam-engine worked monotonously up and down, like the head of an elephant in a state of melancholy madness. (HT, p. 22)

Coketown is "a dense formless jumble" (HT, p. 110), a city of "Towers of Babel" (HT, p. 80), an "ugly citadel, where Nature was as strongly bricked out as killing airs and gasses were bricked in," a "labyrinth of narrow courts upon courts, and close streets upon close streets . . . an unnatural family, shouldering, and trampling, and pressing one another to death" (HT, p. 63). The Gradgrindery—"Stone Lodge," which is a "matter of fact home" (HT, p. 9)—is the ironic complement to Coketown. Both are built upon and governed by the principles of utilitarianism. Descriptively, Coketown is directly representative of the madness of the world. Mr. Gradgrind's establishment, however, and the "system" upon which it is run, represent the triumph of utilitarian order: it is a "great square house," of "very regular feature"; it has the look of a "calculated, cast-up, balanced, and proved house" (HT, p. 10) and is as firm as the "philosophy" of facts. But all the windows of Stone Lodge prove to be "stone blind" (HT, p. 217), and the children learning "fact, fact, fact" in this factory become like the piston-driven "melancholy mad elephants" (HT, p. 111) of the Coketown factories,[1] and the socioeconomic "order" of utility is proved inadequate and fallacious.

There are two main characters who carry Dickens's argument against these worlds: Stephen Blackpool, who works in the factories of Coketown, and Sissy Jupe, child of a circus rider, who first attends Mr. Gradgrind's school and then lives in the Gradgrind house. Stephen sees the world—Coketown, the only one he knows—as "a muddle," "aw a muddle," over and over again (HT, pp. 149-51, 272-73). The "muddle" is Stephen's metaphorical characterization of the madness of the world which Dickens elsewhere represents mythologically as "wilderness," "labyrinth,"

---

1. The schoolmasters are all made in a "factory," too (HT, p. 8).

"maze," and "mud." The only way out of the "muddle," Stephen insists, is by "drawin' nigh to fok, wi' kindness and patience an cheery ways," with "loves and likens" (HT, p. 151). Otherwise, he says, this world will be a "muddle" "till th' Sun turns t' ice . . . till God's work is onmade" (HT, p. 151). He dies, hoping that "th' world may on'y coom toogether more, and get a better unnerstan'in' o' one another" (HT, p. 273).

Sissy Jupe is another of Dickens's "principle of Good" characters, incorruptible in a world of corruption, who exercises a powerful influence merely by her presence. In his notes for chapter 14 of book I, Dickens wrote, "Carry on Sissy—Power of affection."[2] Sissy is not just good; she is goodness. Dickens is not concerned with her being good, but with her being itself, which is a materialization of the "principle of Good." This makes her a horror as a character, and it warps Dickens's thinking and his imagination of her so much so that at the end of the novel he gives her a stock of children—the principle of Good always leads to the principle of Love—without even bothering to give her a husband!

Dickens believes that "there [is] a love in the world," and "that it [has] a way of [its] own of calculating or not calculating" (HT, pp. 292-93)—that it will out, and discover itself. Mrs. Gradgrind learns this through Sissy, and at her death tells Louisa that "there is something—not an Ology at all—that your father has missed, or forgotten." She "don't know what it is" but it is love, just as the unnamed invention in *Little Dorrit* is love. The influence of Sissy has taught Mrs. Gradgrind this great truth, and she has "often sat, with Sissy near me, and thought about it" (HT, p. 199). Mr. Gradgrind receives the same treatment from Sissy, and is converted shortly after his wife's death. He has earlier sensed "that there was something in this girl which could

2. Manuscript, p. 3, Forster Collection, Victoria and Albert Museum, London.

hardly be set forth in a tabular form" (HT, p. 92), and now he realizes "that some change may have been slowly working about me in this house, by mere love and gratitude, that what the Head had left undone and could not do, the Heart may have been doing silently" (HT, pp. 223-24). In the end Louisa too has learned this through Sissy. She even triumphs over James Harthouse, who "cannot say . . . that I have any sanguine expectation of ever becoming a moral sort of fellow, or that I have any belief in any moral sort of fellow" (HT, p. 233). But "with a blending of gentleness and steadiness that quite defeated him" (HT, p. 233), Sissy requires him to leave Coketown, "ridiculous" and "ashamed of himself" (HT, p. 236).

Sissy is the simple child from Sleary's Horse-Riding; and the circus, as it is introduced, creates another dimension of interest for *Hard Times*. The horse-riding is Dickens's curious choice for representing the attitudes and values of art in the novel. When Louisa and her brother are first caught looking at it, Mr. Gradgrind says, "I should as soon have expected to find my children reading poetry" (HT, p. 17). The circus people live at "Pegasus's Arms" (HT, p. 28), though they are always drunk or half-drunk, and the inn itself is "as shabby, as if, for want of custom, it had itself taken to drinking, and had gone the way all drunkards go, and was very near the end of it" (HT, p. 27). The leader of the circus, Mr. Sleary, lisps. It is as though Dickens is unsure of the power of art to do or change anything. In the midst of this strong rhetorical sermon against Benthamism, he seems unable to believe that we can respond to art "with delight, with entertainment, with instruction" (DC, p. 872), or that the artist has indeed a "power of doing good" (DC, p. 843). But this doubt is acknowledged only in Dickens's description of Sleary—his lisp, the circus, drunkenness, the toppling inn of poetry—not in what he actually says. In the chapter entitled "Philosophical," Sleary argues "that there ith a love in the world, and not all Thelf-interetht after all," and "that [love] hath a way of ith own of calculating or not calculating" (HT, pp. 292-93). His conclusion is: "People mutht be amuthed. They can't be alwayth a learning, nor yet they can't be alwayth a working, they ain't made for it. You *mutht* have uth, Thquire. Do the withe thing and the kind thing too, and make the betht of uth; not the wurtht" (HT, p. 293).[3] Both "orders" of the world are challenged by Sleary's thesis: the working world of Coketown, and the Benthamite school world of the Gradgrindery.

Earlier in the novel, in talking about the working class and their lives of drudgery, Dickens warns:

> Utilitarian economists, skeletons of schoolmasters, Commissioners of Fact, genteel and used-up infidels, gabblers of many little dog's eared creeds, the poor you will have always with you. Cultivate in them, while there is yet time, the utmost graces of the fancies and affections, to adorn their lives so much in need of ornament; or in the day of your triumph, when romance is utterly driven out of their souls, and they and a bare existence stand face to face, Reality will take a wolfish turn, and make an end of you. (HT, pp. 162-63)

That is revolutionists' talk. It is repeated at the end of the novel just before the peroration, as he writes of Louisa's "trying hard to know her humbler fellow-creatures, and to beautify their lives of machinery and reality with those imaginative graces and delights, without which the heart of infancy will wither up, the sturdiest physical manhood will be morally stark death, and the plainest national prosperity figures can show, will be the Writing on the Wall" (HT, p. 299).[4] Then, in those last sentences, he

---

3. In "Shakespeare and Newgate," *Household Words*, 4 October 1851, Dickens argues that "the business of life" and its "realities . . . are not and never can be all-sufficient for the mind," and that "sound rational public amusement is very much indeed to be desired." Harry Stone claims that this belief in "amusement" is one of Dickens's "most deeply held beliefs, a central theme in his championship of literature and imagination" (*The Uncollected Works of Charles Dickens* [London, 1970], 1, p. 343).

4. The "Writing on the Wall" is an indirect reference to the destruction

urges us to follow this best example, in order to save ourselves and our world:

> Dear reader! It rests with you and me, whether, in our fields of action, similar things shall be or not. Let them be! We shall sit with lighter bosoms on the hearth, to see the ashes of our fires turn grey and cold. (HT, p. 299)

This is the end of the sermon. The lessons of the story told in it are that love is the only thing that can save us, and that art and the works of the imagination, however strange and impractical and useless they n y seem, are intimately connected with the life of love.[5] Deprived of "the graces of [the] soul" and "the sentiments of [the] heart," life is but "the state of conscious death," Louisa tells her father (HT, p. 216). And the image she chooses with which to conclude her complaint to him is the image of Eden and its default: "What have you done, father, what have you done, with the garden that should have bloomed once, in this great wilderness here" (HT, p. 216). Neither utilitarian theory, nor Gradgrindism, nor the symmetry of Stone Lodge is capable of doing anything to order the wilderness, and that is the point of the novel. Dickens is more simply straightforward here than anywhere else in his fiction, asserting that love is the only constructive alternative to this chaotic postlapsarian world in which we live. He insists that this love is and must remain individual and uninstitutional, a way of life to be undertaken "as part of no fantastic vow, or bond, or brotherhood, or sisterhood, or pledge, or covenant, or fancy dress, or fancy fair; but simply as a duty to be done" (HT, p. 299).

---

of Babylon, and turns this remark back to the revolutionary warning quoted above.
  5. Love and the artist's imagination are connected in *Martin Chuzzlewit* and *David Copperfield* also—ironically, in the case of Pecksniff, who is a loveless man, and a false architect.

2

A Tale of Two Cities is another fable. This time, however, Dickens chooses a larger historical mythology for the setting and the theme of his novel, probing now not a socio-economic "system" or philosophy, but the total construction by which we live, called civilization. *A Tale of Two Cities* is Dickens's tale of the French Revolution; but it doesn't tell the tale in order to elucidate that historical past, or because he is interested in it as a past. The French Revolution is Dickens's symbol, momentarily, for the chaotic present world, pushed to the moment of crisis. And the symbol quickly becomes myth, in Dickens's association of the Revolution as crisis with calamity of the Deluge and the uncertain world of the Creation. Thus the historical novel is turned into a doubly-intense mythic tale, and its story becomes the usual Dickens story of how to survive in this world. The way to survive is always love, in all of Dickens's novels; in *A Tale of Two Cities* he seems to have set out to demonstrate how love is finally a radically better means of changing the world and ordering the chaos than revolution is.

The central story of this short novel is only incidentally related to the French Revolution as an historical event. Sydney Carton and Charles Darnay are the principle characters, and the theme of their story is another variation on the bildungsroman. Carton begins as a useless young man; in the end his selfless sacrifice for Lucie Manette saves him, here as well as hereafter, and he becomes a man. His earlier "dream, that ends in nothing, and leaves the sleeper where he lay down" (TTC, p. 144) is transformed by his final act of heroism into a prophetic vision, fulfilled for "generations hence" (TTC, p. 358).

This vision of Carton's which ends the novel has nothing to do with the Revolution, except as it is brought on by the approaching crisis of his death and, more importantly, as it contains Dickens's answer to the chaos of the Revolution. The Revolution comes about of necessity; and Dickens acknowledges the necessity, just as he has warned of it in *Bleak House, Little Dorrit,* and *Hard Times,* and will repeat the warning in *Our Mutual Friend.* But Dickens does not accept the violence of the Revolution. His impulsive desire to blow things up in *Pickwick Papers, David Copperfield,* and *Bleak House,* the riots and fires of *Barnaby Rudge,* and the constantly recurring mythological reference to the Deluge are all calamitous responses to the need for change. But they are not solutions to the chaos, and Dickens never tried to make them so. In *A Tale of Two Cities* he presents this kind of violence—violence offered against the chaos—more fully than in any other novel, and makes clear both the limits of his tolerance for such and the quiet revolution which he prefers in its stead. The political and public revolution in this novel is the crazy one of "Liberty, Equality, Fraternity, or Death" (TTC, p. 234), and all of the action is carried on—perhaps misleadingly—as though it were but a part of this historical madness. But the private and metaphysical revolution which takes place in the life of Sydney Carton, and which is utterly different from that violent revolution, even though his story is connected to it and built on its events, is the key to the theme of the novel. Carton's revolution comes from his learning to love; and his calm approach to death at the hands of the revolutionary mob is Dickens's representation of the transcendent order to be won by love.

Thus the central story of the novel—of Carton-Darnay and the Manettes—is integrated with its historical, symbolical, and mythical setting. The story could have been created separate from the Revolution, and given a different setting, but it is not. In the end, the resolution of the story becomes for Dickens the resolution of the myth and its question of how to survive this world.

A Tale of Two Cities is more like *Barnaby Rudge* than any other of Dickens's novels. Again, and even more so here, Dickens is using an historical context to represent his mythic comprehension of the world. The two novels even begin from

119

the same time—1775—though from different events. The setting of *A Tale of Two Cities* is London and Paris, the two great cities of the world; the time is that of the greatest crisis of social order and civilization in modern Western history, to Dickens's day. Strictly speaking, the French Revolution is the crisis of the class society; but Dickens chooses to deal with it here as the crisis of all human society, which, by its intensity, makes "what we call the World . . . so real" (TTC, III, 9).

This intensity is set in the first paragraph, in its catalogue of extremes:

> It was the best of times, it was the worst of times, it was the age of wisdom, it was the age of foolishness, it was the epoch of belief, it was the epoch of incredulity, it was the season of Light, it was the season of Darkness, it was the spring of hope, it was the winter of despair, we had everything before us, we had nothing before us, we were all going direct to Heaven, we were all going direct the other way—in short, the period was so far like the present period, that some of its noisiest authorities insisted on its being received, for good or for evil, in the superlative degree of comparison only. (TTC, p. 1)

Despite these contrasts and imbalances, the classes who control society insist on the status quo, and take as their faith the godly belief—it is enunciated regularly from "the State preserves of loaves and fishes"—that "things in general were settled for ever" (TTC, p. 1).

Against this shameless faith Dickens presents the Revolution, trying out in its historical guise his own abstractly revolutionary feelings. The revolution he wants, however, is metaphysical and personal, not political or social. In *Barnaby Rudge* he treated Sim Tappertit's revolution with whimsical and comic scorn, despite its promises of "another state of society" (BR, pp. 203, 300, 392). Here he amends the watchword of the Revolution to "Liberty, Equality, Fraternity, or Death"—and knows, and fears, the destruction the Revolution must harvest. He defends "this terrible Revolution," however, against those who would see it "as if it were the one only harvest ever known under the skies that had not been sown—as if nothing had ever been done, or omitted to be done, that had led to it." "Such vapouring," he says, "was hard to be endured without some remonstrance by any man who knew the truth" (TTC, pp. 226-27). He also opposes "extravagant plots for the restoration of a state of things that had utterly exhausted itself" (TTC, p. 226), though he knows that, under the Revolution, "bad aims were being worked out . . . by bad instruments," and that "the claims of mercy and humanity" go unheeded (TTC, p. 231).

In the terms of Dickens's vision, the Revolution only intensifies the chaos that already exists. "Death" and "Revolution" are already "awake" in France in 1775; and "in England, there was scarcely an amount of order and protection to justify much national boasting" (TTC, p. 2). From the beginning Paris is typically a "vile" place; "the jumbled neighbourhood" of its slums holds no "promise . . . of healthy life or wholesome aspirations," but is a "great foul nest," a "heap of refuse," an "uncontrollable and hopeless mass of decomposition" (TTC, p. 34). London is a "wilderness" (TTC, p. 85), France "a wilderness of misery and ruin" (TTC, p. 118). The wilderness breeds revolution, necessarily, and the one is too much like the other to be good. Chaos breeds chaos; and the mad vengeance of the Revolution has its antecedents in the corrupt "majesty of the law" (TTC, p. 2) of prerevolutionary times:

> There could have been no such Revolution, if all laws, forms, and ceremonies, had not first been so monstrously abused, that the suicidal vengeance of the Revolution was to scatter them all to the winds. (TTC, p. 300)

Perhaps the only hope is that destruction will destroy itself, so that a new world can be born.

Dickens's version of the French Revolution is not just historical, of course; it is fictional, and its significance is mythological.

The novel opens in a time setting which is in part descriptively historical and in part mythological in its references. There are echoes of Genesis in "it was the season of Light, it was the season of Darkness" (TTC, p. 1). The first mythological setting in *Bleak House*, with its "mud," "mire," and "fog," in the beginning of the world is repeated here in the "thick mud" and "steaming mist" of the Dover road in chapter 2.[6] As usual, Dickens does not distinguish the original waters from those of the Flood—or Eden, particularly, from Noah's Ark. The introductory suggestions of the first chaos turn quickly to suggestions of the later myth of the Flood. In the times approaching the Revolution, the world is seen as "at sea, and the ship and crew were in peril of tempest" (TTC, p. 30). Later, the Revolution is called "the deluge of the Year One of Liberty—the deluge rising from below, not falling from above" (TTC, p. 259); and in the next paragraph, "days and nights circled as regularly as when time was young . . . the evening and morning were the first day, other count of time there was none" (TTC, p. 259).

The function of the myth is to collapse all time into the crisis of the historical present: "as I draw closer and closer to the end," says Sydney Carton, "I travel in the circle, nearer and nearer to the beginning" (TTC, p. 295). Once "it was always summer in Eden"; now "it is mostly winter in the fallen latitudes" (TTC, p. 123). From the beginning comes the movement toward the end, toward "the Day of Judgment" (TTC, p. 101), "the Last Day" (TTC, p. 210), when according to Dickens's hopes the virtues of "tenderness and delicacy which . . . [are] as old as Adam" (TTC, p. 184) will return.

The myths of the Creation, the Deluge, Christmas, Heaven, are all myths of death and life, of regeneration through death. Dr. Manette is "recalled to Life"—that is the password between Mr.

---

6. And as in *Bleak House*, there are "fogs atmospheric and fogs legal" in *A Tale of Two Cities* (TTC, p. 131).

Lorry and Lucie Manette in the beginning of the novel (TTC, p. 8). At the end, Carton, who "is not to be reclaimed," though "he is capable of good things, gentle things, even magnanimous things" (TTC, p. 198), is reborn, out of "the evil of this time and of the previous time of which this is the natural birth" (TTC, p. 357). His is the "prophetic" vision which closes the novel: Dickens's Romantic vision of the recreating which will follow the "deluge" of the Revolution.

First Carton sees the destruction of the Revolution itself, then, in a phrase whose sense and language are both Shelleyan, he sees "a beautiful city and a brilliant people rising from this abyss" (TTC, p. 357). That is the general vision, the vision of "the World." Its terms are those of the general mythology of recreation, of regeneration in this world—like building an Apocalyptic or Blakean "Jerusalem" in France's "green and pleasant land." The particular vision here in which Carton sees his own salvation is drawn from Dickens's belief in love, which is "as old as Adam" (TTC, p. 184):

> "I see the lives for which I lay down my life, peaceful, useful, prosperous and happy, in that England which I shall see no more. I see Her with a child upon her bosom, who bears my name. . . .
>
> "I see that I hold a sanctuary in their hearts, and in the hearts of their descendants, generations hence. . . .
>
> "I see that child, who lay upon her bosom and who bore my name, a man winning his way up in that path of life which once was mine. . . . I see the blots I threw upon it, faded away. I see him, foremost of just judges and honoured men, bring a boy of my name . . . to this place . . . and I hear him tell the child my story, with a tender and a faltering voice." (TTC, pp. 357-58)

These "generations" of Carton-Darnay (Darnay is Carton's twin and better "self") will save the world. The "foremost of just judges" will redeem the law which governs society, and in so doing will redeem this first Sydney Carton's very life. Because of this—and here is Dickens's faith—Carton can say, "It is a far, far better thing that I do, than I have ever done; it is a far, far better rest that I go to, than I have ever known" (TTC, p. 358).

A Tale of Two Cities looks forward to the last two complete novels of Dickens's career. There are particular connections, in such details as that the seamstress who goes to her death holding Carton's hand, foreshadowing in that gesture and its comfort the whole motif of hands in *Great Expectations*, and Joe Gargery's central thematic statement, that "life is made of ever so many partings welded together" (GE, p. 28). And Carton's "caring for nothing, which overshadowed him with such a fatal darkness" (TTC, II, 13) in his career in the law, is preliminary to the more detailed study of such in the characters of Mortimer Lightwood and Eugene Wrayburn in *Our Mutual Friend*. More largely, as a mythologically conceived novel of Revolution, and in its mythological investigation of what is called civilization rather than just some of its representative institutional aspects, *A Tale of Two Cities* prepared Dickens for *Great Expectations* and *Our Mutual Friend*, which question directly, fully, and insistently, the idea of a class society.

6

GREAT EXPECTATIONS AND OUR MUTUAL FRIEND

1

From the beginning of *Great Expectations* we know that this is an imperfect world. In the second paragraph we are introduced to death in the tombstones of Pip's parents and his "five little brothers." Death is the incomprehensible end to the "universal struggle" of life, and the world is "the marsh country," a "wilderness" (GE, p. 1). Although Pip is not aware of it, the symbolism of this opening scene argues against the possibility of anyone's ever doing anything constructive during the course of this "struggle": the churchyard is "a bleak place overgrown with nettles," and beyond the churchyard is "the dark flat wilderness" called "the marshes" (GE, p. 1). "Nettles, and . . . brambles . . . bound the green mounds" of the churchyard (GE, p. 4) and the principle effort toward ordering the "wilderness" consists of "great stones dropped into the marshes here and there, for stepping stones when the rains were heavy or the tides were in" (GE, p. 4).

Dickens's challenge is to find and justify "Great Expectations" in spite of this "dismal wilderness" (GE, p. 30) of a world afloat in the chaos of Creation or the disaster of the Flood. Young

Pip first attempts to save himself socially, by becoming what is called a "gentleman" and rising above this vulgar chaos. In the society of the civilized world, chaos is assumed to be the logical environment—and perhaps even the actual result—of "commonness," of ungentlemanly existence. But the best person in the novel is Joe Gargery, who is not a gentleman but "a Man"; and in his simple, good life he is the first character to contribute positively to the correct or natural ordering of the world.

Ironically, of course, this world's chaos is the unnatural product of civilization itself, and thus it cannot be escaped by a retreat into manners and good breeding, as poor Mr. Pocket's family demonstrates. Retreat into gentlemanly status is simply another version, for Dickens, of the physical retreat that so many of his early characters practiced when the world became too much for them. One of the points of this novel and *Our Mutual Friend* is that Dickens will no longer allow the fact of the world's disorder to be ignored. The chaos is pervasive; the marshes, Satis House, and London are all "wilderness" worlds (GE, pp. 1, 30, 58, 83, 379). The "highly ornamental, but perfectly helpless and useless" Mrs. Pocket (GE, p. 178) may refer to the blue book all she wants, but her children will still tumble about under and around her in a dangerously disorderly state.[1]

But the example of the Pockets comes much later in Dickens's story—comes, in fact, as Pip is just beginning his attempt to rise above the chaos on "Great Expectations." In the beginning of the novel there is no escape for Pip, no place for him to retreat to, except the forge; and Mrs. Joe, who is "given to government" (GE, p. 53) and bringing up "by hand" (GE, p. 6) is in command there. Another of Dickens's orphans, Pip is alone in the world and helpless. When he is sent to Miss Havisham's for the first time he sees her retreat from the world—which he doesn't under-

---

1. Mrs. Pocket is a kinswoman to Mrs. Micawber in *David Copperfield*, with her "mama and papa" reflections.

stand—more as elegant than as mad. What he sees is "rich," "fine," "gilded," "bright," "splendid," "sparkling" (GE, p. 52). When he reports his experience at Satis House to Joe and Mrs. Joe and Mr. Pumblechook it comes out a wild fantasy of class— a coach, four dogs, gold plates, flags, swords. Pip is not merely infatuated with Estella at Satis House; just as important, he is seduced there by the values of the class society.

Miss Havisham represents the class society by more than her possessions. Her stopped life is symbolic of the attachment of the upper classes—the establishment—to the status quo, and demonstrative of the perversity of that attachment.[2] Of course Miss Havisham's attachment is more to the status quo ante, to be exact. But what she is defending herself against is change; the change that follows "twenty minutes to nine" (GE, p. 53); and Satis House—"whoever had this house, could want nothing else" (GE, p. 51)—is the symbol of the status quo, all "barred" and "walled up" (GE, p. 50). In the end it must be destroyed, like so many instruments of statis in Dickens, because the way of the world is change.[3]

Once Pip sees Satis House and Estella he begins to dream his way out of the chaos of the marshes, not once realizing that the world he dreams of is just as chaotic as the one he knows, and just as badly decayed. To order the world of Satis House he has to tell "lies" (GE, p. 65). It is ironic that he falls in love at Satis House, which is a loveless place. But Pip's love for Estella at this point is pure romantic—erotic—infatuation, one of the few instances of

---

2. In one of his essays Dickens compares "Stoppage and Progress, . . . the exclusive principle and all other principles, . . . perfect Toryism and imperfect advancement," opting obviously for the idea of change. The occasion is a comparison between China (Stoppage) and England (Progress). See "The Great Exhibition and the Little One," *Household Words*, 5 July 1851, in *The Uncollected Writings of Charles Dickens*, 1: 329.
3. Miss Havisham's retreat from life can also be seen in comparison with Miss Betsey Trotwood's retreat to the cottage near Dover in *David Copperfield*. In raising Estella not to love men the jilted Miss Havisham shows us what the divorced Miss Betsey would have done to David if he had really been a girl.

such in all of Dickens's fiction;[4] and Pip has to learn charity, as in his eventual love for Joe, for Magwitch, and for Herbert Pocket, before he can win Estella. This kind of love, for Dickens, is what is necessary for the salvation of the world; curiously, this is the kind of love one makes to produce children. Erotic love is selfish; here it leads Pip into almost disastrous distortions of his life. First he becomes disenchanted—"restless aspiring discontented" (GE, p. 101)—with his condition, and wishes desperately "to get on in life" (GE, p. 68). He sees himself "a common labouring-boy . . . my hands were coarse . . . my boots were thick" (GE, p. 60). "I should never like Joe's trade," he says: "I had liked it once, but once was not now" (GE, p. 99). He is "ashamed of home. . . . it was all coarse and common" (GE, p. 100). Like Little Em'ly in *David Copperfield*, he starts "thinking what I would buy if I were a gentleman" (GE, p. 109), and whines to Biddy of his ambitions to be such (GE, p. 120). Then, newly protected with "Great Expectations" (GE, p. 130), he starts to dream not only of himself changed but of changing, "improving," others; and in doing so he creates "lies" just like those he told about Miss Havisham's house. Pip has been "ashamed" of Joe (GE, p. 95); now he wants to help him "rise in station" to "a higher sphere of life" (GE, pp. 140-41), which means putting Joe in "wrong . . . clothes" (GE, p. 212).

Pip's plan is in part generous, but it is still wrongheaded; the problem of the world is not Joe's social station, or Pip's, and the world can't be changed by a change in either. Joe, after all, is "only master of [his] own trade" (GE, p. 148), and a "natural . . . Man" (GE, p. 267); he is what he is supposed to be, and is

---

4. David Copperfield falls "in love" with Miss Shepherd, Miss Larkins, and Dora; Uriah Heep has his lewd red eye on Agnes; Steerforth seduces Little Em'ly; James Harthouse tries to seduce Loo Gradgrind; John Harmon loves Bella Wilfer "against reason"; Eugene Wrayburn has Lizzie Hexam "in his power," and Bradley Headstone is obsessed with his passion for her. For the most part, however, there is little erotic love in Dickens's world; mostly love is charity, which makes brother-sister relationships out of marriages.

capable of good works. But Pip, seduced in his youth by class consciousness, loses hold of his very being. Thus the problem with his life is not social, as he thinks it is, but a problem of "metaphysics" (GE, p. 65); and Joe's advice, as his "true friend" (GE, p. 66), is that Pip be true and real, that he quit his "lies" (GE p. 66). The world needs people like Joe, and it needs people like what Pip can become, for its salvation. The kind of gentleman Pip plans to be—and is, for most of the latter part of the novel—does not at all suit. Joe is a better man than Pip, always; Herbert is a truer gentleman than Pip in every way; and even Magwitch, for all of his pride in being the "owner" of a gentleman (GE, p. 306), in having "made a gentleman on" Pip (GE, p. 304), is a more genuine, honorable man than Pip. Pip has learned class, the social substitute, for love, the metaphysical reality which for Dickens can save the world. Now he has to unlearn the selfish escapism of class and discover this generous kind of love. Then, in the end, he will deserve to win Estella, for whom he started his career in society and lies.

Both Pip and Estella have changed at the end, and this change is what the novel is about. Both of them learn finally Dickens's kind of love, which is what legitimizes their reward in each other and consequently makes the second conclusion to the novel the appropriate one. For both of them, change has come through adversity and adversity's teaching; that "suffering has been stronger than all other teaching" (GE, p. 460) is the one significant line which occurs in both conclusions. Suffering is what brings them in contact with the world as it is: a suffering world. Pip's disappointment and sickness are the world's disappointment and sickness; the perversion and cruelty practiced on Estella are the same the world at large suffers from regularly at the hands of society. From what they learn through suffering—"I feel thankful that I have been ill," says Pip (GE, p. 446)—they learn to love, and to do what Dickens's love must do—which is begin to remake the world as it should be made.

All of the places of the novel are "wilderness." The marshes are constantly in a "confusion . . . of mist" and "mud" (GE, p. 14); Satis House is a "rank garden . . . overgrown with tangled weeds" (GE, p. 58), a "neglected garden" (GE, p. 74), a "heap of decay" (GE, p. 82), and a "ruined place" (GE, p. 380); London is "ugly, crooked, narrow, and dirty" (GE, p. 153), a "shameful place" (GE, p. 155) full of "the dingiest collection of shabby buildings" and "dismal houses . . . in every stage of dilapidated blind and curtain, crippled flower-pot, cracked glass, dusty decay. . . . soot and smoke. . . . [and] rot" (GE, pp. 162-63), a "wicked place" where you "may get cheated, robbed, and murdered" (GE, p. 161), and altogether "a frouzy, ugly, disorderly, depressing scene" (GE, p. 246). The world itself is in adversity. In terms of the Genesis myth—in items of "rank garden" and "rot," of "crippled flower-pot" and "tangled weeds," of "confusion," "mist," "mud," and general "disorder"—Eden is no longer Paradise, and the Flood is at hand. In this darkest of Dickens's mythic moods, the hulks, prison ships out in the river off the marshes, are the only "Noah's Arks" (GE, pp. 36, 217), and they are "wicked" ones at that. When Pip discovers that Magwitch, who escaped from one of those hulks, is his patron, the false ark of society upon which Pip has sailed with his gentlemanly expectations falls apart and sinks altogether: "I began fully to know how wrecked I was, and how the ship in which I had sailed was gone to pieces" (GE, p. 307). Continuing the same metaphor, it is Herbert who saves Pip from drowning after this shipwreck—Herbert, who has earlier been Pip's "anchor," without whom he will "soon be driving with the winds and waves" (GE, p. 395)—by engaging him to work as a clerk for his merchant shipping firm.

Work is necessary after the Fall. The world is a world of death and disorder, requiring for its improvement work and love. At "the end of the first stage of Pip's expectations" (GE, p. 152), as Pip prepares to leave the village for London, "the light mists

[are] solemnly rising, as if to show [him] the world" (GE, p. 251). There are several changes of horses along the way, and then as he approaches the city, "the mists had all solemnly risen . . . and the world lay spread before [him]" (GE, p. 152). These lines suggest, as Edgar Johnson has pointed out,[5] Milton's lines at the end of *Paradise Lost* on the expulsion of Adam and Eve from Paradise:

> as Ev'ning Mist
> Ris'n from a River o'er the marish glides,
> . . . .
> The World was all before them, where to choose
> Thir place of rest, and Providence thir guide:
> They hand in hand with wand'ring steps and slow,
> Through *Eden* took thir solitary way. (12. 629-49)

Earlier, Michael has told Adam and Eve that if they can have "Love," they need not worry "To leave this Paradise, but shalt possess/ A paradise within thee, happier far" (12. 583-87). This idea of the postlapsarian world to be reordered by love is the thesis of Dickens's mature philosophy; and although no one actually makes Pip such a promise as Michael's to Adam and Eve, *Great Expectations* still fulfills it in its conclusion. Pip and Estella go

> out of the ruined place; and, as the morning mists had risen long ago when I first left the forge, so, the evening mists were rising now, and in all the broad expanse of tranquil light they showed to me, I saw no shadow of another parting from her. (GE, p. 460)

There is no retreat, and the happiness-ever-after must be read in the context of the imperfect place where they will live.[6] The

---

5. *Charles Dickens: His Tragedy and Triumph* (New York, 1952), 2:993-94.
6. In this novel "retreat" (GE, p. 196) means to "cut off the communication" (GE, p. 195), which means to cut off love. Wemmick's is the retreat so de-

world is not restored to perfection; but living in the world is changed by love, and in Dickens's faith, change is almost always for the better.

Joe, the "master of [his] own trade" (GE, p. 140), the stable character around whom change revolves, has always known the value of love, and his forge has been symbolic of love's strength. Joe is always ready when he is needed. He is "ever the best of friends" (GE, p. 44), a "true friend" (GE, p. 66) who combines "strength with gentleness" (GE, p. 133). Pip says of Joe: "It is not possible to know how far the influence of any amiable honest-hearted duty-going man flies out into the world; but it is very possible to know how it has touched one's self in going by" (GE, p. 101). Joe's best advice to Pip is in his richly paradoxical forge metaphor, "life is made of ever so many partings welded together" (GE, p. 212), which is the epitome of Dickens's adversity-teaches-love theme.[7] In *Our Mutual Friend* Dickens sings "the bright old song . . . that oh, 'tis love, 'tis love, 'tis love, that makes the world go round" (OMF, p. 671)—and the spinning and the singing signify, perhaps, something like the harmony of the spheres (harmony being a regular metaphor in that novel) made by love. In *Great Expectations* he has Pip sing the song of the forge, which is much the same thing:

> Thus, you were to hammer boys round—Old Clem! With a thump and a sound—Old Clem! Beat it out, beat it out—Old Clem! With a clink for the stout—Old Clem! Blow the fire, blow the fire—Old Clem! Roaring dryer, roaring higher—Old Clem! (GE, p. 89)

Ironically, the song is introduced into the novel not as it is sung at the forge, but as Pip sings it for Miss Havisham and as they sing it together while he wheels her around her room.

---

scribed, though curiously, he makes a sort of love to Miss Skiffins there. But then the castle is only a make-believe retreat; really, anyone could step across "a chasm four feet wide, and two deep" (GE, p. 195).

7. This definition of life as love is much like Teilhard de Chardin's metaphor of love as the attraction of particles through the long evolution from atoms to humans.

When Pip finally learns to love he loves Joe, and Magwitch, and Herbert, and then is reunited with Estella. Pip's downfall comes from his first infatuation with Estella, and from his anxiety to be a "gentleman" for her. He is given "Great Expectations," and is seduced and perverted by them. Both Magwitch and Pip want Pip to become a gentleman, because that is what the class society says is the enabling purpose of money: making gentlemen. In becoming a gentleman, Pip becomes as perfectly "fit for nothing" (GE, p. 224) as he should be, and then is as shocked and revulsed as is socially proper when Magwitch turns up as the origin and source of his fortune. Through all of this, of course, he gets no closer to winning Estella. Part of the problem is Estella —but part of it is also Pip. What is wrong is that Pip has misinterpreted the idea of having "Great Expectations" from the beginning. In assuming that it takes money to make a gentleman, and that a fortune is a great expectation, Pip submits himself to society's perversion. The greatest expectation anyone can have in Dickens's world is the expectation of love. Near the end of the novel, as Pip recovers himself from his distraction, gives up his prosperous future, and learns to love poor Magwitch, this "varmint" finally becomes Pip's true benefactor. Pip's "repugnance to him [is] all melted away," and he sees "in the hunted, wounded, shackled creature who held my hand in his . . . a man who had meant to be my benefactor, and who had felt affectionately, gratefully, and generously, towards me with great constancy through a series of years" (GE, p. 423); and he promises Magwitch, "I will be as true to you as you have been to me" (GE, p. 424).

Magwitch has never been a bad man—and for this we should recall Pip's and Joe's simple hopes for his escape during the chase on the marshes in the beginning of the novel. Magwitch has always been a victim, of society and of the corrupt world over which society presides. Significantly, he is the namesake of the first victim, Abel, the son of Adam (GE, p. 328). Dickens presents him for our sympathy as a man acted upon by adversity rather than one who makes his own misfortune. In this Magwitch is linked to Pip, too, who is constantly suffering at the hands of others; and thus from their opening meeting in the churchyard on the marshes—where all of Pip's family lies buried—Magwitch is Pip's father. Magwitch has "been soaked in water, and smothered in mud, and lamed by stones, and cut by flints, and stung by nettles, and torn by briars" (GE, p. 2), and in general always acted upon; he is "a wretched warmint, hunted . . . near death and dunghill" (GE, p. 16). Brought up to be a "warmint" (GE, p. 311), he has "been done everything to" (GE, p. 328). Thus Dickens excuses him for whatever he has done, and for the "warmint" role in life he has been required to play.

In Dickens's vision we are all largely influenced by our environment; and what we mean by environment in a modern world like Dickens's is society. Thus the "universal struggle" (GE, p.1) of life, in which Pip and Magwitch in particular are involved, becomes a battle for survival in the wilderness of civilization. "Death," for example, haunts Magwitch in the form of a hanging threat from his childhood until he dies in Pip's arms in prison; and the child Pip—so much his symbolic father's son—is obsessed with a fear of being hanged for his innocent offenses against adult social authority.

That most of Dickens's characters are related to their environment is due largely, I think, to what I have postulated as his creative method: first he sees the world, and it takes particular form, mythically and symbolically, before him; then out of the matter of this vision he creates his characters, who take their form and their being from its reality. This theory does not account for a few of the evil—or mean—people, like Compeyson in *Great Expectations*, nor does it explain the essentially good people. In many of the novels—in *Oliver Twist*, *The Old Curiosity Shop*, and *Dombey and Son* in particular—there is one person, a "principle of Good" character, who is neither tainted nor endangered by the world, and whose goodness is both incomprehensible and irrelevant. In *Great Expectations* there is no such character. Herbert Pocket, in his guilelessness, is probably the closest to "pattern" goodness (BH, p. 852), but he is more like the innocent Tommy Traddles in *David Copperfield*, and thus more interesting. Joe is good; but his goodness is natural rather than preternatural, and honest rather than pious.

Herbert Pocket first appears as "the pale young gentleman" (GE, p. 84), "so brave and innocent" (GE, p. 85), in the garden at Satis House. When Pip meets him next, in London, he is "still a pale young gentleman" whose figure looks "as if it would always be light and young" (GE, pp. 167-8). He seems to Pip to have "a natural incapacity to do anything secret and mean," and has "something wonderfully hopeful about his general air" (GE, p. 167). Herbert's ambition is to be "a capitalist—an Insurer of Ships" (GE, p. 173); and though he doesn't become exactly this, he does become a partner in a merchant shipping firm, through Pip's generous assistance. Herbert's business is as important for Pip as his friendship, and in a sense they are almost the same. When Pip can no longer pretend to gentlemanly expectations, he has to face the emptiness and uselessness of his life: "I have been bred to no calling, and I am fit for nothing" (GE, p. 324). The "Harmonious Blacksmith" (GE, p. 168)—it is from this "charming piece of music by Handel" that Herbert gets Pip's new name— has broken his apprenticeship at the forge for nothing. But Herbert takes Pip on as a clerk in the shipping business and as a partner in his family, where he lives "with Herbert and his wife" (GE, p. 455) for more than ten years.

It is in this life with Herbert that Pip learns what love—Dickensian love—really is. As Herbert proposes to leave England on business, he apologizes to Pip for going "when you most need me," and Pip replies, earnestly, "Herbert, I shall always need you, because I shall always love you" (GE, p. 436). Love is what holds our lives as well as our world together; and when Pip and Herbert shake hands on this and on other serious occasions, they weld themselves together in need and in love. The same idea is expressed in Joe's great line, "life is made of ever so many partings welded together" (GE, p. 212). Love is the weld; without it, our lives fly apart, disintegrating into atoms of self and other. What Dickens wants is a united life, a united world. On an individual level this unity is what makes "a Man," like Joe; on a general level it transcends the divisions of a class society and gives a real order and harmony to civilized life. Occasionally we see men like Joe in Dickens's novels, and in our own lives; we can only hope—with Dickens—that some day someone will see that other, larger unity organize the world.

Near the end of *Great Expectations*, Joe and Biddy, and Herbert and Clara are married. Joe has been Pip's brother-in-law, and Biddy now becomes in effect his sister. Herbert has been a brother to him throughout their stay in London, and for a number of years after leaving England Pip lives with Herbert and his wife as a part of their family. When Pip returns to England, he tells Biddy that he is "so settled down in [the Pockets'] home" and is such "an old bachelor" that he can't think of getting married (GE, p. 457). But being a bachelor in Dickens's world is a disadvantage, to say the least. All of the novels end with marriages and families. Dickens's pattern for suggesting the change and progress which will make a new world is to have the hero marry and raise a family. Pip should marry Estella. They have both learned, through "suffering," what love is. Pip is now a better man, and Estella has been "bent and broken, but . . . into a better shape" (GE, p. 460). Symbolically they are already related as brother and sister now: Magwitch was Pip's "second father" (GE, p. 304), and Estella turns out to be his real daughter. But they are no longer passionate young people. At the end Pip says, "We are friends"; and Estella answers, "And will continue friends apart" (GE, p. 460). Then Pip concludes the novel:

> I took her hand in mine, and we went out of the ruined place; and, as the morning mists had risen long ago when I first left the forge, so, the evening mists were rising now, and in all the broad expanse of

tranquil light they showed to me, I saw no shadow of another parting from her. (GE, p. 460)

We can read this conclusion either of two seemingly contradictory ways. We can read the last paragraph as Pip's picking up their love with his strength and carrying them to the happiness they both deserve, so that they do not in fact "continue friends apart," but live together as lovers. Or we can read Estella's last remark as in a very real sense final. Pip then remains a bachelor, and the value to be appreciated in his life is friendship, the basic charitable kind of love which Dickens always values highly, and often confuses with romantic love. But there is still that final paragraph—after Estella's remark—for us to deal with. To understand the conclusion of the novel we must resolve her words with those with which Pip ends his narrative: "I saw no shadow of another parting from her." These words take us back through Pip's and Estella's conversation about "parting" to Joe's great, echoic line, "life is made of ever so many partings welded together" (GE, p. 212). Joe is referring to life in an imperfect world, of course. And as Pip and Estella go "out of the ruined place" as the "evening mists [are] rising" they become Adam and Eve after the Fall. But they go out into the world with the faith— at least Pip seems to have it—that their love is strong enough to weld their lives together even though they are apart. What this conclusion means for Dickens—and it takes us back to *David Copperfield,* where he began *Great Expectations,* after all—is that life in this world can be held together, in unity and in order and in love, by the imagination of the author. Love can overcome the chaos, even though the chaos still remains.

2

The chaos certainly remains in *Our Mutual Friend.* We see even less of the unity of the world or the order of life in this novel than we saw in *Great Expectations. Our Mutual Friend* is a larger novel, broader in its perspective and more inclusive in its focus than *Great Expectations*; and in it we see more of the chaos that Dickens always sees, and more of society and its sham. Things are bad from the beginning, and they hardly change for the better. Chapter the Last shows us society acting as it always does and always had, in a classic feast of Podsnappery. True, the several chapters previous to this have meted out a great deal of justice and happiness, and at the end there are valiant promises all round of "turning to ... in earnest" (OMF, p. 812) to retrieve the natural order of the world from societal disintegration. But those "turning to" are young men—Eugene Wrayburn, Mortimer Lightwood, John Harmon—and they have much hard work ahead of them if they are to make any significant changes. They have rescued themselves—that takes place in the body of the novel—but rescuing the world is a different matter. The Veneerings, the Podsnaps, Lady Tippins, Buffer, Boots, and Brewer are still in number the predominant members of this world, and they gather formidably in the final chapter to sound in monotonous and monumental unison "the Voice of Society" (OMF, pp. 815-20).

The prospects for relief from this awful, cacophonous voice are in the work that Eugene promises to do, and in his marriage to Lizzie Hexam; in the "power of doing good" (OMF, p. 680) which John and Bella Harmon have in their fortune; and in the small, comic classlessness of the Boffin version of society. Mortimer, however, remains a bachelor, and in the last chapter returns to "Society," to take another look at it. His response to it is what concludes *Our Mutual Friend*; and this response reveals to us his true role in the novel and his final importance for Dickens.

Mortimer ends the novel "shak[ing] hands with [Mr. Twemlow] cordially ... and far[ing] to the Temple gaily" (OMF, p. 820). Mortimer's gaiety comes from what he knows is going to happen to the world, thanks to Eugene and Lizzie and John and Bella, and from the courage this knowledge has given him to respond with energy and self-assertive sincerity to the outrages of

Podsnappery. His gaiety also comes from seeing the sudden heroism with which Twemlow opposes society and its basic idea of class, even in the presence of this heavy establishment. It is as though in this last chapter of *Our Mutual Friend* Dickens is trying to show us the revolutionary changes that can actually take place in our world once change gets started. Rather than leave us with Eugene and Lizzie and John and Bella good and happy and married—his usual conclusion, if we add some children to complete the symbolic prophecy of the picture—he lets Mortimer take us back into the world which these good people must work against.

Mortimer is a curious, shadowy character to be intrusted with this task. As a bachelor he is at best an incomplete figure in Dickens's world. An unhappy solicitor, a bored, frustrated, and uncommitted young man waiting to find himself, he is never directly involved in the action of the novel in any of its various plots. His main role is that of storyteller—to "Society," strangely. In the beginning he tells the story of "the man from Somewhere," which becomes the Harmon story, and introduces Eugene to Lizzie. In the end he tells the story of Eugene's and Lizzie's marriage. Everything else in the novel happens in the context of these two stories. By his telling them, Mortimer relates them and their sub-plot connections to the world of society which they challenge; and by his telling them to the Veneerings and Podsnaps and their kind, he makes the challenge out of the story, and becomes, thus, as story-teller, the primary antagonist to "Society."

Mortimer's first story—of the man from Somewhere and his alleged drowning—contains nothing in it to threaten society, though Mortimer's way of telling it is generally critical of the social requirement of accumulating money. And as the Harmon story is developed in the novel, the social ideal of money is rejected in favor of the human ideal of love;[8] and in the end, the

---

8. The "marriage" of Alfred and Sophronia Lammle is a parodic play on the relationship between love and money in Dickens's world.

ascendancy of John and Bella is a direct threat and challenge to the world that attends the Veneering dinners. The story of the man from Somewhere also introduces Eugene and Lizzie, and their chance introduction is what makes Mortimer's second story. For the most part Mortimer's experience of the novel is in his observation of these stories, and it is this observation-experience which changes him. By the final chapter, when he goes back to Veneering's and tells his second story, he is much more openly critical—even defiant—of society and of the civilization it pretends to make.

> "Say, how did you leave the savages?" asks Lady Tippins.
> "They were becoming civilized when I left Juan Fernandez," says Lightwood. "At least they were eating one another, which looked like it." (OMF, p. 816)

An inquisition into the marriage follows. Lizzie is identified by society as "a female waterman" and "a factory girl," and Mortimer counters that she is Lizzie, who has "rowed in a boat with her father" and "had some employment in a paper mill" (OMF, p. 817). A vote is taken, and Eugene is condemned by all present—except Twemlow, who suddenly finds his strength, and stands up for Lizzie and Eugene and for himself. He insists on calling Eugene a "gentleman" and Lizzie a "lady," and in so doing attacks Veneering society and Podsnappery at its very base. He insists on using the word "gentleman . . . in the sense in which the degree may be attained by any man" (OMF, p. 820), thus denying the idea of a class society.

Twemlow's outburst—and for this previously trembling little man it is an outburst of his self—breaks up the Veneering party. As "the company disperse . . . Mortimer sees Twemlow home, shakes hands with him cordially at parting, and fares to the Temple gaily" (OMF, p. 820). Mortimer's gaiety comes from his awareness that things are changing, or at any rate are capable of changing, for the better. And in some sense he must know, for

Dickens, that change comes as a result of a certain kind of instruction, that the story he has told has been received by Twemlow, at least, "with delight, with entertainment, with instruction" (DC, p. 872).

One of the indications of Mortimer's peculiar status as observer in *Our Mutual Friend* is that he doesn't have any of the adversity traumas the other characters all have. There is a larger group of young men in this novel than in any other of Dickens's works, all of them trying to grow up. In addition to John Harmon, Eugene, and Mortimer, there are more minor figures like Bradley Headstone, Charley Hexam, Fascination Fledgeby, and young Sloppy. Three of this group—Harmon, Eugene, and Headstone—drown or almost drown. Mortimer observes them all.

The primary action of *Our Mutual Friend* is drowning or nearly drowning. It is the adversity which so many of the characters face. In Dickens's other novels the world is often threatened with the Flood, or sits on the brink of the third day of Creation, when the land and the waters were first separated. Here, however, drowning belongs not just to the mythic dimension of the novel, but to the immediate and particular dimensions of the action and plot as well. Individuals drown, or almost drown—not the world. John Harmon and Eugene Wrayburn almost drown; Gaffer Hexam drowns in the Thames, and Rogue Riderhood and Bradley Headstone drown together upstream in Plashwater Weir Mill Lock; George Rayfoot finds a watery grave, as have all the bodies Gaffer and Riderhood fish from the river; and even Silas Wegg is drowned symbolically, as he is excused from the novel by Sloppy's dropping him into a scavenger's cart "with a prodigious splash" (OMF, p. 790). What all of this means is that in this last complete novel Dickens creates his mythic world actually in the lives of individual characters rather than as a separate world generally or universally congruent to the particular world of the action. Myth and story are united here; it is as though Dickens is testing the population of the Ark, to see if any of them can swim it on his own. Edgar Johnson speaks of *Our Mutual Friend* as "that dust-heap of modern civilization from which mankind must strive to be reborn,"[9] which is true; but my point is that in this novel Dickens sees modern civilization as destructive of individual lives, and that he concentrates first, then, on the salvation of individuals rather than the rebirth of mankind.

The opening of *Our Mutual Friend*—"In these times of ours, though concerning the exact year there is no need to be precise" (OMF, p. 1)—suggests a mythic expansion of the present. The first thing we see is "a boat of dirty and disreputable appearance," which is "allied to the bottom of the river rather than the surface, by reason of the slime and ooze with which it was covered, and its sodden state" (OMF, p. 1). This perverse boat—an anti-Ark, perhaps—tows behind it the body of John Harmon's substitute, supposed to be our mutual friend. In chapter two Mortimer tells the Harmon story at a party at the Veneerings', concluding with the information of the drowning carried over from the first chapter. In Mortimer's bored speech small words like "the" often disappear, and thus the death of the mysterious "man from Somewhere" is announced generically rather than specifically: "Man's drowned" (OMF, p. 17). "Man" is drowned: it is as though in this general or representative time, and in this representative, symbolic world, all of us are liable to drowning.

But "Man" is not drowned; individual men are drowned or almost drowned, saved or not saved, changed or not changed. The liability is universal, but instances are particular. As usual, Dickens becomes obsessed with his imagery—here, that of drowning—and by introducing it promiscuously throughout the novel he makes it work as a thematic and mythic metaphor. Not only do many people drown or nearly drown; Charley Hexam speaks of "Pharaoh's multitude, that were drowned in the Red Sea"

---

9. *Charles Dickens: His Tragedy and Triumph* 2: 903.

(OMF, p. 19); the Veneerings converse with their dinner guests as though they were drowning men—"he plunged into the case, and emerged . . . with a Bank Director," and she "dived into the same waters for a wealthy Ship-Broker, and . . . brought him up, safe and sound, by the hair" (OMF, p. 134); Mortimer and Eugene think it might "be exciting to look out for wrecks" along the river (OMF, p. 145); Eugene feels "half drowned" from being in the vicinity of the Thames (OMF, p. 164), and after his attack and near-drowning his slow recovery is characterized as the "frequent rising of a drowning man from the deep, to sink again" (OMF, p. 740); and Bradley and Rogue discuss "being drowned" (OMF, p. 636) the first time they meet at Riderhood's lock. Drowning is a test, literally and mythically. Literally, it is an adversity-conversion mechanism; mythically it tests individual Noahs and their ability to stay afloat.

There are a number of boats in *Our Mutual Friend*—Gaffer Hexam's, Rogue Riderhood's, Mortimer's and Eugene's, the ship that John Harmon arrives on, boats of various kinds upriver on the Thames, and boats and ships downriver, to Greenwich and elsewhere. The Ark, however, actually appears twice: in a remark of Charley Hexam's about "the mud that was under the water in the days of Noah's Ark" (OMF, p. 28), and in the death of little Johnny, to whom Bella gives a "Noah's ark" (OMF, pp. 326, 328-29) complete with "All Creation" lined up "in pairs" to enter (OMF, p. 329). Charley's reference to the Ark is not particularly meaningful, except as it introduces this central Dickensian myth to the novel. Little Johnny's toy is more important. Noah's family of animals is paralleled with the "family" of sick and helpless children in the hospital, whom Johnny sees as "all . . . brothers and sisters of his" (OMF, p. 329); momentarily this "family whom God had brought together" are like "All Creation" looking for Noah and his saving Ark. When Bella Wilfer is converted from her avarice, she looks forward to her marriage to John with the phrase "I see land at last" (OMF,

p. 617). As she and John are the central characters in the primary story of the novel—he is "Our Mutual Friend"—they become its central mythic characters as well, and to "see land at last" means something like seeing Mount Ararat from the Ark. For them, then, the voyage is over.

The resolution of the Harmon story, with Bella's becoming "true golden gold" (OMF, p. 772) and marrying John and freeing her father from the horrible dues of Mrs. Wilfer, is the only completed resolution in the novel. In the end John has the Harmon fortune and is alleged to be using it in the best benevolent way. The money has "turned bright again, after a long rest in the dark, and [is] at last beginning to sparkle in the sunlight" (OMF, p. 778). Bella is rich, in money and in love, and being rich has "a great power of doing good to others" (OMF, p. 680). She and John take over the duty of benevolence from Mr. and Mrs. Boffin and seem no longer to have any problems with anything. Indeed, everything seems so complete and final and fulfilled with them that they seem almost to be retiring into the middle of the world, despite Dickens's protestations that they are active people and that their goodness is active goodness. Mrs. Boffin is an example of why Dickens creates benevolent people: as John says of her, "Some among us supply the shortcomings of the rest" (OMF, p. 332). John defines benevolence again in discussing individual purpose with Bella: "No one is useless in this world . . . who lightens the burden of it for any one else" (OMF, p. 520). We all need "some sustaining purpose" in life (OMF, p. 525); that John and Bella are supposed to have this and act upon it at the end of the novel we must take upon faith, it seems.

But for Eugene and Lizzie and for Mortimer nothing is completed or settled. They are not rich, and they still have the world to contend with. When we see them last, Eugene and Mortimer are just beginning to "turn to in earnest" (OMF, p. 812) and work in the world; but we can much more easily accept the reality of their working than we can that of John and Bella. This is partly because Eugene and Mortimer are realized as characters more than John. John carries out an elaborate ruse of becoming himself, from Handford through Rokesmith to Harmon, but remains still something of a fabrication, a theoretical character; whereas Eugene and Mortimer actually go through the process of becoming, and as they do we learn to accept them as real people. They begin the novel bored, uncommitted to anything, including themselves, and unhappy with their professions in the law. Eugene calls himself "a bad idle dog" (OMF, p. 235) who has spent "a trifling, wasted youth" (OMF, p. 754). Both he and Mortimer have always been ready to engage themselves, but have never found anything worth the effort, either in their work with the civilizing law or in their life in society. "But show me a good opportunity," says Eugene, "show me something really worth being energetic about, and *I'*ll show you energy" (OMF, p. 20). Lizzie is what Eugene finds "worth being energetic about," and his love for her helps him discover "a mine of purpose and energy" in himself (OMF, p. 754). As a bachelor in society Eugene's greatest effort "towards self-improvement" has been the keeping of an unused kitchen full of "household implements" whose "moral influences," he says, will teach him "domestic virtues" (OMF, p. 295). Married to Lizzie, he must give up this game and turn his "energy . . . to the best account" (OMF, p. 754). His marriage—a marriage of love, duty, and debt—is an affront to society, of course, a violation of the code of class. Eugene considers retreating with Lizzie "to one of the colonies, and working at [his] vocation there," but rejects this retreat as "wrong" (OMF, p. 812). Then he and Mortimer resolve together to "turn to in earnest" in this world, to work to set it right. And setting it right means in part opposing the class system, which is one of the causes, for Dickens, of the world's chronic disorder.

This hard realism is not present in the Harmon story. What Dickens does in that part of the novel is a bit of comic alchemy, his last piece of miracleworking, in which he turns money into gold and gold into love. One of the first things Bella says is, "I love money, and want money—want it dreadfully" (OMF, p. 37); later she calls herself "the most mercenary little wretch that ever lived in the world" (OMF, p. 319). She doesn't know that money is dust, until Noddy Boffin, "the Golden Dustman," shows her by pretending to be corrupted by it. There is good in Bella, and she is beautiful, but her "head [is] turned" (OMF, p. 598). John Harmon falls romantically in love with her much like Pip does with Estella—"I cannot help it," he says; "reason has nothing to do with it. I love her against reason" (OMF, p. 372)—and little Johnny bequeaths "a kiss for the boofer lady" (OMF, p. 330) at his death. Lizzie, too, sees good in Bella, and in their exchange of confidences causes a softening and a change in her. "I feel as if whole years had passed since I went into Lizzie Hexam's cottage," she says; "I feel as if much had happened—to myself, you know" (OMF, p. 530). Lizzie is a model for Bella; her love is that selfless love, charity, which Dickens always preaches. Until Bella can convert to this kind of love, it is useless for her to love or be loved in the erotic or romantic sense. Lizzie has told her that hers is a "heart that, once won, goes through fire and water for the winner, and never changes" (OMF, p. 529). When she learns selflessness—and it is learning the "truth" of her "soul," we are told (OMF, p. 775)—she alchemizes, and turns "true golden gold at heart" (OMF, p. 773) and thus can withstand the "trials" (OMF, pp. 679, 745, 752) that John sets in "proving" (OMF, p. 370) her.

The crisis of Bella's conversion comes at Mr. Boffin's firing John to save her from his "affections and hearts and trumpery" (OMF, p. 596). She cries:

> "Oh, Mr. Rokesmith, before you go, if you could make me poor again! Oh! Make me poor again, Somebody, I beg and pray, or my heart will break if this goes on! Pa, dear, make me poor again and take me home! I was bad enough there, but I have been so much worse here. Don't give me money, Mr. Boffin. . . . only let me speak to good

146

little Pa, and lay my head upon his shoulder, and tell him all my griefs. Nobody else can understand me, nobody else can comfort me, nobody else knows how unworthy I am, and yet can love me like a little child. I am better with Pa than any one—more innocent, more sorry, more glad!" (OMF, pp. 596-97)

This outburst is a kind of catharsis for Bella. From it comes her acceptance of John as her lover: "I am yours if you think me worth taking" (OMF, p. 606). Bella is purged of all the dross of her being, and her true mettle is discovered. She is "gold" now, and John knows that he is "rich beyond all wealth" in having her (OMF, p. 680). As R. W. tells him, Bella "brings you a good fortune when she brings you the poverty she has accepted for your sake and the honest truth's" (OMF, p. 608). At their wedding Dickens turns the whole world gold momentarily, in pathetic sympathy with their love: there is a general "golden bloom" on Greenwich (OMF, p. 667) and the wines they drink are "golden drinks . . . bottled in the golden age" (OMF, p. 668); as they turn homeward at the end of the day it is by "a rosy path which the gracious sun struck out for them in its setting" (OMF, p. 671).

Throughout *Our Mutual Friend* there is a conflict between money, the gold that is dust, and love, the gold that is true riches. Jenny Wren tells Lizzie that her love is "more to be relied upon than silver and gold" (OMF, p. 234). Mortimer mythologizes Old Harmon—who loved no one—as a man who "lived in a hollow in a hilly country entirely composed of Dust" (OMF, p. 13). In his will, Old Harmon tries to turn marriage into a financial contract for John and Bella, which is the same thing Eugene's father tries to do for him (OMF, p. 146).[10] There has long been "old rust and tarnish" on the Harmon fortune (OMF,

10. The Lammles marry for money; and Fascination Fledgeby's mother married his father, a moneylender, only when she was "unable to pay" her debt to him (OMF, p. 268), thus bringing Fledgeby into the world as the result of a bad debt.

p. 372)—which proves that it is not true gold—and it has been the breeder of much unhappiness. Money is foul, generally; "The Treasures of a Dunghill" is the biography of a man whose life was "avarice and dirt," and whose fortune was a "rich piece of manure," and who "warm[ed] his dinner by sitting upon it" (OMF, p. 482). Yet money can be "turned bright again" with generous use, and "after a long rust in the dark" can begin at last "to sparkle in the sunlight" (OMF, p. 778). In this "pretty and promising picter" (OMF, p. 778) money gives one "a great power of doing good" (OMF, p. 680).

Everyone needs money; it is one of the basic "realities" of life (OMF, p. 321). Betty Higden needs a "loan . . . of twenty shillings to fit out a basket" (OMF, p. 383); Sloppy has to have a job, to "make a man and a workman" of him (OMF, p. 391); and John Harmon needs the small "fortune in the waterproof belt round [his] body" (OMF, p. 371) in order to carry out his careful scheme. Only Mortimer and Eugene profess to reject money, but what they reject is their inheritances and allowances, not the money they will earn once they are pledged to work, in "turning to at last" (OMF, p. 812). There are of course many people who want money too much; and in their avarice they are incapable of love. The Lammles' marriage is a terrible farce, because they want money. Fascination Fledgeby cannot become a man—cannot reach puberty (Pubsey and Co.), cannot find a girl, cannot love Georgiana Podsnap—because he loves money so much. Silas Wegg lusts after money, and has a wooden-legged orgasm reading about it, and falls into a "pecuniary swoon" (OMF, p. 483). Mr. Venus, obviously a lover, wins Pleasant Riderhood over to his suit only after he quits his avaricious partnership with Wegg.[11] The desire for money and the virtue of love just don't

---

11. Mr. Venus is an interesting character. His vocation is "articulation," putting together whole skeletons from the "various" pieces he has. Wegg is such an unnatural creature that his leg bone, which Mr. Venus owns, won't fit any model "miscellaneous" skeleton. Wegg's worth, according to Mr. Venus, is "as a Monstrosity" (OMF, I, 7).

go together. Early in the novel Mr. Boffin tells Mortimer that "there's some things that I never found among the dust" (OMF, p. 91)—and what he refers to, surely, is love. But for most of us love is not one of the everyday "realities" of life like money is. It is Bella who calls "poverty and wealth" the "realities," and "love," she says, is no more real than "fiery dragons" (OMF, p. 321). Though Dickens argues that love is more real and more enduring than money, he has no way of making love appear in the novel with the same impressive physical reality that money has. So what he does is transfer the imagery of one to the other, and make love into "true golden gold" (OMF, pp. 772, 773), "a most precious and sweet commodity . . . that never was worth less than all the gold in the world" (OMF, p. 683). Gold is good, but not all money is gold; in the hands of those who hoard it— and hoarding is the status quo, again—it tarnishes and rusts, like only false gold would do. True gold shines, in use. Love is the same for Dickens. Selfish love is not true love; generous love, the love that involves "giving [one]self up to another" (OMF, p. 392) is the true love, and it makes one rich.

The truth or falsity of substances is perhaps the main question in *Our Mutual Friend*. Again, it is not so much the world itself which Dickens questions now, but individuals. Dickens knows that there is no real Eden any more, so he does not try to fabricate the place and call it real. Mr. Riah has his "little garden" (OMF, p. 278) on the roof of Pubsey and Co., made up of a "few boxes of humble flowers and evergreens" (OMF, p. 279); but it is surrounded by "the encompassing wilderness" (OMF, p. 279), and is neither in this world nor in this life—"so high," as Jenny says, "you feel as if you were dead" (OMF, p. 281). Pleasant Riderhood dreams of "Eden" in terms of "far-off islands," as an alternative to the real world she knows in Limehouse Hole with its "reeking street" (OMF, p. 351); and under the influence of love John Harmon sees a steamboat on the Thames as "gold-dusty" rather than "coaly" as it really is (OMF,

p. 664). But Dickens knows that the basic substance of the world is "dust" and "mud," over and over again, and that the state of things in it is chaotic. The world at large is a "jumble" (OMF, pp. 61, 215), a "wilderness" (OMF, pp. 61, 70, 279). There is one small, precariously situated oasis of order in the center of the chaos, at Miss Abbey Potterson's pub, the Six Jolly Fellowship-Porters. Architecturally "The Fellowships" is "a narrow lop-sided wooden jumble . . . with a crazy wooden verandah impending over the water," encroached upon by "a wilderness of court and alley" (OMF, p. 61). The tavern stands "dropsically bulging over the causeway" (OMF, p. 27), and is "all but afloat at high water" (OMF, p. 61). Still, it is "the Fellowships," and inside it is an orderly place: "It has been hard work," Miss Abbey says, "to establish order here, and make the Fellowships what it is" (OMF, p. 69). The order established here—by "hard work" —matches Dickens's dream that it is "love that makes the world go round" (OMF, p. 671).

But the Fellowships is not Eden, and what order it maintains is isolated, simple, and small. Generally speaking, love is hardly to be found. Everyone must feel as Twemlow does "the unvanquishable difficulty of existence" (OMF, p. 9). The time now is after the Fall. We are in the world of "Cain" and "Abel" (OMF, p. 713), and it is difficult sometimes to tell which of them is which. Everything—and everyone—in the novel is a question of substance; "What, what, what? Who, who, who?" is the cry, and we all must look for "the genuine article" (OMF, pp. 118-19). Most of the falseness is in some way attributable to the social environment, and thus it is at the first great dinner at the Veneerings' that "the Analytical Chemist" is introduced, questioning "what it's made of" (OMF, p. 10). The genuine articles, "made" true, are Mrs. Boffin, who is "a lady, and a true one, or there never was a lady born" (OMF, p. 203); Mr. Boffin, who is "good and generous . . . the best of men" (OMF, p. 465) despite his seeming "change" (OMF, p. 475); and Lizzie, whom the Voice of

Our Mutual Friend

Society tries to deride by calling her a "female waterman, turned factory girl" (OMF, p. 817) until Mortimer makes clear the difference between what she does and what she is. Bella is so corrupted by her love of money and the social position it will buy her that she would "sell [her] very nature. . . . if [she] could get enough of it" (OMF, p. 472). Her "head [has been] turned" (OMF, p. 598), and she does not know herself (OMF, p. 531). In the end, "the truth . . . of her own weak soul" (OMF, p. 775) is worked out, and she assumes her "natural" ways (OMF, p. 808) as a good, "true" Bella. Eugene waits, like the chronically bored Mortimer (OMF, p. 88), "to begin life" (OMF, p. 97). Various people give him good advice—to work, after the example of the bees, as Mr. Boffin suggests (OMF, pp. 93-94), to "turn industrious" as Jenny Wren advises (OMF, p. 238); but the Eugene Wrayburn who exists at this point can't possibly follow such advice—"Who knows what he is doing, who is careless what he does" (OMF, p. 240). All the advice is moral advice, and just as helpful as the "moral influences" of Eugene's kitchen (OMF, pp. 289, 295). Eugene's problem is that he doesn't know who he is. He knows that the first question he must ask, before he can ever undertake to decide what he is doing, is the metaphysical riddle of himself: "Eugene Wrayburn. . . . Riddle-me, riddle-me-ree, perhaps you can't tell me what this may be" (OMF, p. 295). He is not a "good" man (OMF, p. 692), and cannot act "morally" (OMF, p. 237) until he comes into himself; then, however, he is "a true man" and can follow "the right course" (OMF, p. 742)—can marry Lizzie, can "turn to in earnest" (OMF, p. 812).[12]

There are other characters in *Our Mutual Friend* who are metaphysically corrupted by society. Many critics have discussed the technique of dehumanization which Dickens uses. What I

---

12. When Mr. Boffin is pretending to be a miser, he talks several times of his changed "self" (OMF, pp. 464, 475).

wish to point out is the meaning of dehumanization in the context of the whole novel: the dehumanization of characters is corruption of their being—and this is caused by the corrupting environment of the class society. Petty avarice and worship of his social connection (with Uncle Parker, Aunt Jane, Master George, and Miss Elizabeth) are already turning Silas Wegg to wood when we meet him. Mrs. Wilfer's haughty jealousy of class is what makes her such an unnatural wife and mother; she looks "like a frozen article on sale in a Russian market" (OMF, p. 612), and has "a cheek . . . as sympathetic and responsive as the back of the bowl of a spoon" (OMF, pp. 310-11) or like "a cool slate for visitors to enrol themselves upon" (OMF, p. 611). The Veneerings' assumption of class with all its "high varnish and polish" is what makes them "a trifle sticky" (OMF, p. 6) to the touch; and they, like the Lammles, are as false as their names. Twemlow and Lady Tippins are also more objects than people, Twemlow as "an innocent piece of dinner-furniture" (OMF, p. 6) and Lady Tippins as a camouflage lady with "an oblong face, like a face in a tablespoon, and a dyed Long Walk up the top of her head" (OMF, p. 10). Lady Tippins gets worse; but Twemlow, who once says of himself that he is "even a poorer man of business than [he is] a man" (OMF, p. 569), recovers both his humanity and his manhood in the end, when he supports Lizzie and Eugene.

Mr. Podsnap is not corrupted by money or society in exactly the same way these other characters are. Rather, he is the image —a brazen calf of cumbersome public proportions—which they worship, and honor with their emulation. Society takes the name of its "religion," the worship of wealth, from this "representative man": "Podsnappery" (OMF, p. 129). He prescribes its "articles of faith," and interprets Providence for the faithful. As creator, strangely, his primary work is not to create, not to allow, not to acknowledge the existence of anything that would disturb the small static universe of his understanding. He is first presented "clearing the world of its most difficult problems, by sweeping them behind him," for he allows "nothing else To Be—anywhere" (OMF, pp. 128-29) that does not please him. In the religion of Podsnappery anything "disagreeable" is removed "from the face of the earth" (OMF, pp. 141, 627) and declared not to exist. It is in this self-inflicted blindness that Podsnap's corruption lies. He is the chief representative of the class society, the archprotector of the status quo, which in its narrowness and its rejection of change is a misguided, selfish dreamer's retreat.

Even Eugene and Mortimer are dehumanized, in a sense, by society. They are so bored, so utterly enervated by the falseness of life in society, that they lose their natural vitality and energy as "young men" (OMF, p. 20). Their response to society keeps them from being themselves; they are so overwhelmed with dismay that they retreat, defensively, into nonexistence. Not only are they not their true selves, then; more terribly, they are hardly anybody at all. Seated at Veneering's table, Mortimer "won't talk"; Eugene sits "buried alive in the back of his chair," and awaits the passing of "the champagne chalice" as though it is a poison cup (OMF, p. 11). Mortimer looks out from under his "drooping eyelids" and thinks, "What's the use" (OMF, p. 11); Eugene starts to talk, seems to be "coming out," but "goes in again" instead (OMF, p. 12). This false world is so depressing that it seems to them impossible to live in it. It is his depression, perhaps, that makes Mortimer announce the death of the mythic "man from Somewhere" in terms so universal: "Man's drowned." For all the hope that Mortimer and Eugene feel, "Man" might as well be drowned. But Dickens won't accept their pessimism, and pushes them both back toward life—toward courage and strength and energy. He won't let them retreat from the world, because retreat means death; and they are young men, potential heroes, who must live and work in the world for change.

153

"Everything that happens," Dickens wrote, "shows beyond mistake that you can't shut out the world."[13] In the end of *Our Mutual Friend* he is more true to this thesis than anywhere else in his fiction. He does not shut out the continuance of evil, as the last chapter with its Veneering feast shows; nor does he let the Voice of Society shut out the fact of change, either—change as represented by Twemlow's sudden heroism in defending Eugene's and Lizzie's marriage, change as represented by that marriage itself. Dickens does not pretend that the world at the end of the novel is in any way an ideal one; but then it is not absolutely dark, either. There is work to be done in it, and there is love in it. Together, these are enough to justify, for Dickens, the novel's final word, "gaily."

We can all go into the world of the future "gaily," provided we go with love in our hearts and an understanding that "the degree [of gentleman] may be attained by any man" (OMF, p. 820), provided we go into the world to "mingle with it, and make the best of it, and make the best of [ourselves] into the bargain,"[14] Each of us has to be saved to save the world; there is no magic that can do it all at once, "All Creation" is personified in each Noah, and the hope for tomorrow lies in the vision that can unite and order this large family. The Voice of Society— the voice of "the froward and the vain"—makes its "usual uproar" (LD, p. 826) here the same as it did at the end of *Little Dorrit*; but there is work underway to change the world for the better in spite of them. The world as it is, Dickens says, is at "a pass impossible of prosperity, impossible of continuance" (OMF, p. 503). There must be a revolution: but not a bloody one, like the French and the Americans had in their histories, because Dickens knows that their dreams failed, and they did not really change anything; and not just a mythic one, like the Flood, be-

---

13. Dickens to Wilkie Collins, 8 September 1858.
14. Ibid.

cause the new society built from the family of another Ark will fail just like the old one did. The revolution Dickens wants is that which will take place within each individual. His revolution will take place as "metaphysical" change and will reveal in each changed man his "true self" (D&S, p. 477). On this rock Dickens would build a world.

CONCLUSION

ICKENS'S VISION GROWS A GREAT DEAL MORE SERIOUS BE-
tween the opening of *Pickwick Papers*, with Mr. Pickwick's "Observations on the Theory of Tittlebats" (PP, p. 1),
and the conclusion of *Our Mutual Friend*, with Mortimer listen-
ing critically to "the Voice of Society." The comedy of Pickwickian innocence turns through many phases, until finally it
turns to caustic criticism of Podsnappery and its egocentric ig-
norance. One of the ways to follow this change is through close
attention to the way Dickens presents the world to himself,
imaginatively. He looks at the world, and by "the blending of
experience and imagination" (DC, p. 665) he begins to see it,
not just as it is but also as it signifies mythically. The mythic
dimension of Dickens's novels surrounds the world of the action.
It creates the meaning of his fiction, by being its vision.

This vision does not come to Dickens all at once, of course;
most likely it never became a part of his conscious awareness.
He knew, surely, his own growing critical response to life in
England and the state of human affairs; but the translation of
this response through his imagination into the mythic organization of his art seems to have been mostly unconscious.[1] It is from

---

1. Dickens may even have been aware that he worked unconsciously. In a
letter he wrote to Sheridan Le Fanu on 26 May 1890, he warned his fellow-

156

this unconscious imagination that Dickens's greatness comes; and as it develops his work becomes both larger and more coherent. The quaint comedy of Mr. Pickwick's "Speculations on the Source of the Hampstead Ponds" is dwarfed by the large and thematic mythic meditations on the Deluge which replace Mr. Pickwick's little essay in the later novels.

By concentrating on the way Dickens uses Genesis mythology we come to see more clearly both his definition of the world as "mad," and the possible ways of dealing with it. His obsession with the chaotic aspects of his mythology—the third day of Creation, the Deluge, and Babel—make a more clear and meaningful kind of social criticism than the direct and particular criticism which derives from the plots of the novels or is spoken by their narrator. Just as King Charles's head is Mr. Dick's "allegorical way of expressing" his knowledge of the world's madness, so the crises of Genesis mythology are Dickens's way of representing the chaos which obsesses him. In the early novels he uses Eden and Noah's Ark as solutions to the chaos. The trouble with these solutions is that they are only mythical; and in proposing them as solutions to the problems of the real world, he leads his characters into unreality. The chaotic side of Genesis mythology matches the real world as Dickens sees it, and the connection between the world of his experience and that which his imagination mythologizes from the chaos is both impressive and true. But although there is an Eden in Genesis, and Noah's mythical family is saved from the Deluge, there is no Eden in the world of Dickens's experience, and the flood waters of that real world will never recede by themselves to allow some Noah to start us off anew.

Through the course of his career Dickens teaches himself that

---

novelist that "no story should be planned out too elaborately in detail beforehand, or the characters become mere puppets and will not act for themselves when the occasion arises." This letter was first published by Bert G. Hornback, in "Five New Dickens Letters" in *The Michigan Quarterly Review*, 10: 4 (1971), 255-60.

we have to live in this real world; that we can't escape or retreat or retire from it. There are no Edens left where we can go to be safe and innocent again. We must be responsible to our experience, and use our imagination to find real solutions to our problems. We must admit that what once was Eden is now a "wilderness," a "ruined garden"; that what was simple is now a "labyrinth," a "maze"; and that we must set to work to order it all again, to make that old dream of order real again. Eden is as irrelevant as Heaven, because neither of them solves the problems of this life in this real world.

As Dickens learns to deny himself Eden and Heaven, he also learns to see the inadequacy of Noah and his Ark as a response to the chaos of the Deluge. The Ark is another retreat; and when Noah is boarded up there he can exercise no influence at all on the waters that surround him. In the early novels, Noah is the mythic model for all the benevolent men, beginning with Mr. Brownlow; his task is to protect all those who are entrusted to his care, by taking them out of the flood. As Dickens becomes aware of the inadequacy of retreat as a solution to the problem of our chaos, he also learns that the protective paternalism of Noah is wrong. If we are to change this world, we all need strength. We all must learn to swim in the flood, to save ourselves in this world.

Babel is another sign of our confusion, one whose continuing mythic effect on our lives is more immediately apparent, perhaps, than is that of the Deluge or the expulsion of Adam and Eve from Paradise. For Dickens the tower of Babel is the monument at the center of our civilization; it is the fabulous repository of our archives. Babel appears by name in seven of Dickens's novels, and by interpolation can be seen in most of the rest. The reference to Babel is critical of industry in *Dombey and Son*, *Bleak House*, and *Hard Times*; of government in *David Copperfield*; and of the general confusion that is London in *The Old Curiosity Shop*.[2] In *Martin Chuzzlewit* General Choke suggests

---

2. See A Concordance of Dickens's Mythology, p. 173 below, for these references.

to Martin that England "has piled up golden calves as high as Babel, and worshipped 'em for ages" (MC, p. 349)—which seems to be a criticism of the whole of English culture. In the opening chapter of *Little Dorrit* Dickens catalogs a dozen different nationalities, "descendants from all the builders of Babel," coming to Marseilles to trade (LD, p. 1); and then he writes a novel about the universal lack of communication which comes from Babel, and what this lack causes. This is the most comprehensive and revealing use of Babel in the novels, and the one which is closest in its sense to those uses which I want to propose by interpolation.

We are at Babel, for Dickens, because we can't talk correctly, because we can't communicate. Communication frequently means love in Dickens's world; and noncommunication or false communication—lying—means chaos. Thus the Workhouse in *Oliver Twist* is an institution modeled after Babel, with its lies to Christianity engraved upon its walls, just as much as the Circumlocution Office is in *Little Dorrit*. M'Choakumchild's school in *Hard Times* is a Babel Factory in the way it teaches utilitarian jargon. The Court of Chancery is Babel in *Bleak House*, and the lawyers all speak its incomprehensible dialect. The Reverend Mr. Chadband speaks in a tongue learned at Babel, too, as he goes about in *Bleak House* perverting truth into "terewth"; and other false ministers, like the Reverend Mr. Stiggins in *Pickwick Papers* and the Reverend Melchisedech Howler (of "the Ranting persuasion") in *Dombey and Son* are also graduates of that confusing school. Politics is always seated at Babel in Dickens's world, and politicians always speak its language. In *David Copperfield* Mr. Dick's full name is Richard Babley, but he can't stand to be called by it because, as Miss Betsey says, "he has been ill-used enough by some that bear it, to have a mortal antipathy for it" (DC, p. 201). The name "Babley" has a larger meaning than this, however; the words "Babel" and "babble" are related, both linguistically and in Dickens's imagination; and Mr. Dick's strange name is the name of his—and our—family madness, against which he complains in his "Memorial." Finally, in *Our Mutual Friend*, the whole cacophonous chorus of "the Voice of Society" is from Babel, and it is against them that Mortimer tells his stories.

That the good people in Dickens's world have to grow up among and learn to work against such forces as Babel, the Flood, and the aboriginal chaos of the Creation indicates how oppressive was his sense of the universal confusion of the real world. As Dickens sees the world, from midway through *Pickwick Papers* until the very end of his career, things are so absolutely bad, and mad, that the Babel edifice called civilization is about to "come rushing down and bury us alive." We are "at a pass impossible of prosperity, impossible of continuance" (OMF, p. 503). Faced with such a crisis, Dickens first suggests retreat, and then, in the later novels, revolution. But the revolution he proposes is not public, or social, for that way lies a new madness, like "Liberty, Equality, Fraternity, or Death" (TTC, p. 234). Dickens's revolution is personal and metaphysical; it requires that each of us change individually. The slogan for this revolution is "that bright old song, that oh, 'tis love, 'tis love, 'tis love, that makes the world go round" (OMF, p. 621).

Social critics from John Ruskin to George Bernard Shaw to, most recently, Charles Reich in *The Greening of America* have been aware of the importance of Dickens's understanding of our world's madness. Too few critics, however, have taken seriously Dickens's philosophy of love—"Carol philosophy," as he sometimes called it—as an answer to this madness. Perhaps it has seemed too simple, or simplistic. Yet it is as serious and substantial as Romanticism or Christian idealism, and is developed, as they are, out of the logic of the imagination. As Dickens formulates his philosophy through such basic, essential mythology as the Book of Genesis it asserts its own significance as a comprehension of life. We are never very far away from the beginning —from the Creation, Eden, the Deluge, and Babel—in trying to find out where we are now, and where we must go from here. What Dickens does is redefine the relevance of these mythic times for us, through the power of his imagination. As he grows through his career, he comprehends more of the meaning of this mythic world and sees more clearly thus how life must be lived in the real world. And his simple philosophy of love becomes more substantial and more compelling.

Almost a century after Dickens's death Adlai Stevenson said, in his last public speech,

> We travel together, passengers on a little space ship, dependent on its vulnerable reserves of air and soil; all committed for our safety to its security and peace; preserved from annihilation only by the care, the work, and I will say the love we give our fragile craft. We cannot maintain it half fortunate, half miserable; half confident, half despairing; half slave to the ancient enemies of man, half free in a liberation of resources undreamed of until this day. No craft, no crew, can travel safely with such vast contradictions. On their resolution depends the survival of us all.[3]

I don't know whether Stevenson read Dickens or not, but their metaphor is the same; and Stevenson's use of it, in a modern form, helps to clarify Dickens's use of it and the final meaning of his mythology. Dickens's Ark, which in the early novels seemed to be the one from Genesis, saving the good people from God's Flood, turns out to be the ship on which all of us Noahs "travel together"; and the only way for us to save ourselves from drowning is to love each other. Love, for Dickens, is "the highest wisdom ever known upon this earth" (ED, p. 107). By loving each other we can save "All Creation" (OMF, p. 329).

---

3. Speech at Geneva, Switzerland, 9 July 1965.

A CONCORDANCE FOR DICKENS'S MYTHOLOGY

THESE REFERENCES ARE TO THE BEST OF MY KNOWLEDGE complete, except that I have not recorded each instance of certain usages, like Miss Flite's "Day of Judgment" in *Bleak House*, when the phrase is used several times in one short conversation, or "Eden" as the name of the American settlement in *Martin Chuzzlewit*. The first three subdivisions—the Creation, Eden, and the Deluge—are the most important. Part IV, Babel, is also a part of the Genesis mythology; part V, Judgment Day, is, of course, apocalyptic. Part VI, Wilderness, is related to the Genesis mythology as Dickens's one-word ritual description of the chaos of the beginning of the world, the world after the fall of Adam, and the time of the Flood. Parts VII and VIII record the use of two words, Maze and Labyrinth, almost synonymous with Wilderness in Dickens.

I. *The Creation*

"Never was such a dinner as that, since the world began" (NN, p. 817).

"A flat morass . . . where the very trees took the aspect of huge weeds, begotten of the slime from which they sprung, by the hot sun that burnt them up" (MC, p. 376).

"Let us see the natives in their aboriginal condition" (Steerforth, DC, p. 302).

"As much mud in the streets, as if the waters had but newly retired from the face of the earth, and it would not be wonderful to meet a Megalosaurus, forty feet long or so, waddling like an elephantine lizard up Holborn Hill" (BH, p. 1).

"Beginning the World" (Chapter title, BH, p. 864).

"I am very weak, sir, but I hope I shall be stronger; I have to begin the world" (Richard, BH, p. 865).

"It might perhaps have been objected that the William Barnacle wisdom was not high wisdom or the earth it bamboozled would never have been made, or, if made in a rash mistake, would have remained blank mud" (LD, p. 406).

"It was the best of times, it was the worst of times . . . it was the season of Light, it was the season of Darkness" (TTC, p. 1).

"Though days and nights circled as regularly as when time was young, and the evening and morning were the first day, other count of time there was none" (TTC, p. 259).

"For, as I draw closer and closer to the end, I travel in the circle, nearer and nearer to the beginning" (Mr. Lorry, TTC, p. 295).

II. *Eden*

"The ball-nights at Ba-ath are moments snatched from Paradise; rendered bewitching . . . by the absence of tradespeople, who are quite inconsistent with Paradise" (Mr. Dowler, PP, p. 497).

"The house . . . has a large garden, and is situated in one of the most pleasant spots near London" (Mr. Pickwick, PP, p. 796).

"People sometimes call these dark yards 'gardens'; it is not supposed that they were ever planted, but rather that they are pieces of unreclaimed land, with the withered vegetation of the original brick-field" (NN, p. 8).

"But, the faint image of Eden which is stamped upon [our hearts] in childhood, chafes and rubs in our rough struggles with the world, and soon wears away" (The grey-haired gentleman's tale, NN, p. 57).

Smike "spoke of beautiful gardens, which he said stretched out before him, and were filled with figures of men, women, and many children, all with light upon their faces; then, whispered that it was Eden—and so died" (NN, p. 763).

"But care and suffering . . . are devils, sir—secret, stealthy, undermining devils—who tread down the brightest flowers in Eden" (Gabriel Varden, BR, pp. 198-99).

"No son had ever been a greater comfort to his parents than Abel Garland had been to his" (OCS, p. 110).

The churchyard "was another world, where sin and sorrow never came; a tranquil place of rest, where nothing evil entered" (OCS, p. 401).

Among Kit Nubbles's children "there was an Abel, own godson to the Mr. Garland of that name" (OCS, p. 554).

The Chuzzlewit Family "undoubtedly descended in a direct line from Adam and Eve" (MC, p. 1).

"It is remarkable that as there was, in the oldest family of which we have any record, a murderer and a vagabond, so we never fail to meet, in the records of all old families, with innumerable repetitions of the same phase of character" (MC, p. 1).

"Secondly, and yet without trenching on the Blumenbach theory as to the descendants of Adam . . ." (MC, p. 6).

"Mrs. Gamp had been . . . in attendance upon a ceremony to which the usage of gossips has given the name which expresses, in two syllables, the curse pronounced on Adam" (MC, p. 310).

"More American experiences. . . . Some account of Eden, as it appeared on paper" (Chapter heading, MC, p. 341).

"Impossible for a place to have a better name, sir, than the Walley of Eden. No man couldn't think of settling in a better place than the Walley of Eden. And I'm told . . . as there's lots of serpents there" (Mark Tapley, MC, p. 342).

"Well! . . . and do you think of settling in Eden?" (General Choke, MC, p. 348).

"We are a new country, sir; man is in a more primeval state here, sir; we have not the excuse of having lapsed in the slow course of time into degenerate practices . . . man, sir, here is man in all his dignity" (General Choke, MC, p. 349).

"If we determine on Eden, the business shall be commenced as soon as we get there" (Martin, MC, p. 352).

"Martin's head was two inches nearer the roof of the little wooden office, with the consciousness of being a landed proprietor in the thriving city of Eden" (MC, p. 357).

"Mr. Chuzzlewit . . . had purchased a 'lo-cation' in the Valley of Eden, and intended to betake himself to that earthly Paradise by the next steamboat" (MC, p. 363).

"Scadder is a smart man, and—and—nobody as goes to Eden ever comes back a-live" (Captain Kedgick, MC, p. 373).

"I'm a day's journey nearer Eden, and am brightening up afore I die. . . . p'rhaps by the time I get there I shall have growed into a prophet" (Mark Tapley, MC, p. 374).

"Even Eden, you know, ain't all built" (Mark Tapley, MC, p. 377).

"At last they stopped. At Eden too. The waters of the Deluge might have left it but a week before: so choked with slime and matted growth was the hideous swamp which bore that name" (MC, p. 377).

"We can build the oven in the afternoon. There never was such a handy spot for clay as Eden is" (Mark Tapley, MC, p. 382).

"It is an ancient pursuit, gardening. Primitive, my dear sir; for, if I am not mistaken, Adam was the first of our calling. My Eve, I grieve to say, is no more, sir; but . . . I do a little bit of Adam still" (Pecksniff, MC, p. 384).

"Oh, weary, weary hour! What were the wanderings of Cain, to these" (MC, p. 414).

"From Mr. Moddle to Eden is an easy and natural transition. Mr. Moddle, living in the atmosphere of Miss Pecksniff's love, dwelt . . . in a terrestrial Paradise. The thriving city of Eden was also a terrestrial Paradise" (MC, p. 513).

"Eden for ever!" (Mark Tapley, MC, p. 518).

"It was long before [Martin] fixed the knowledge of himself so firmly in his mind that he could thoroughly discern the truth. . . . Eden was a hard school to learn so hard a lesson in" (MC, p. 525).

"So low had Eden brought [Martin] down. So high had Eden raised him up" (MC, p. 525).

"I don't know this man from Adam" (John Westlock, MC, p. 607).

Jonas Chuzzlewit "looked back . . . to see if his quick footsteps . . . were already moist and clogged with the red mire that stained the naked feet of Cain" (MC, p. 720).

"And can you be a day, or even a minute . . . in the garden of what's-its-name—"
"Eden, I suppose, mama" (Mrs. Skewton and Edith, D&S, p. 287).

"People cannot spare one. But seclusion and contemplation are my what's-his-name—"
"If you mean Paradise, mama, you had better say so" (Mrs. Skewton and Edith, D&S, p. 288).

"The frowsy and uneven patch of ground which lay before [John and Harriet Carker's] house . . . had once (and not long ago) been a pleasant meadow, and was now a very waste" (D&S, p. 474).

" 'Tis woman as seduces all mankind. For which . . . you'll overhaul your Adam and Eve, brother" (Captain Cuttle, D&S, p. 796).

Miss Betsey's lawn at Dover is "a little piece of green. . . . those sacred precincts . . . that hallowed ground. . . . The one great outrage of her life, demanding to be constantly avenged, was the passage of a donkey over the immaculate spot" (DC, pp. 194-95).

"I seemed to pay the deepest attention to him, but I was wandering in a garden of Eden all the while, with Dora" (DC, p. 392).

"Dora, laughing, held the dog up childishly, to smell the flowers; and if we were not all three in Fairyland, certainly *I* was" (DC, p. 396).

"What the mud had been doing with itself, or where it came from, who could say? But it seemed to collect in a moment, as a crowd will, and in five minutes to have splashed all the sons and daughters of Adam" (LD, p. 30).

"Cain might have looked as lonely and avoided" (LD, p. 124).

"A more primitive state would be delicious to me" (Mrs. Merdle, LD, p. 242).

"A shaft of light . . . brought to Clennam's mind the child's old picturebook, where similar rays were the witness of Abel's murder" (LD, p. 267).

"To be sensible of having (as we all have, every one of us, all the children of Adam!) offenses to expiate and peace to make, does not justify the desire to forget" (Mrs. Clennam, LD, p. 356).

"If we were in a more primitive state, if we lived under roofs of leaves, and kept cows and sheep and creatures instead of banker's accounts . . . well and good" (Mrs. Merdle, LD, p. 391).

"The features of the surrounding picture were . . . a number of houses at odds with one another and grotesquely out of the perpendicular, like rotten pre-Adamite cheeses cut into fantastic shapes and full of mites" (LD, p. 490).

"Nobody knew that [Merdle] had any capacity . . . which had ever thrown, for any creature, the feeblest farthing-candle ray of light on any path . . . among the multiplicity of paths in the labyrinth trodden by the sons of Adam" (LD, p. 556).

"Now, from the days when it was always summer in Eden, to these days when it is mostly winter in fallen latitudes, the world of man has invariably gone one way—Charles Darnay's way—the way of the love of a woman" (TTC, p. 123).

"For a moment [Mr. Lorry] held the fair face from him . . . with a genuine tenderness and delicacy which, if such things be old-fashioned, were as old as Adam" (TTC, p. 184).

"Behind the furthest end of the brewery was a rank garden . . . the rank garden was the garden of the house, and . . . it was overgrown with tangled weeds" (GE, p. 58).

"And the mists had all solemnly risen now, and the world lay spread before me" (GE, p. 152; see discussion of this line above, pp. 131-32).

"A few boxes of humble flowers and evergreens completed [Mr. Riah's] garden" (OMF, p. 279).

"For sailors to be got the better of were essential to Miss Pleasant's Eden" (OMF, p. 351).

"Better to be Abel than Cain" (Chapter title, OMF, p. 703).

III. *The Deluge*

"I'm Mister Noah Claypole" (OT, p. 30).

"Free from that cramped prison called the earth, and out upon the waste of waters. . . . the whole scene is madness. . . . the ship in an eternity of troubled water" (MC, pp. 245-46).

"There were English people, Irish people, Welsh people, and Scotch people. . . . to be found in that unwholesome ark "(MC, p. 248).

"Ah! He'd bought the land . . . and paid for it too. Every sort of nateral advantage was connected with it, the agents said; and there certainly was *one*, quite unlimited. No end to the water" (Mark Tapley, MC, p. 282).

The National Hotel, in America, is an "Ark" (MC, p. 358).

"At last they stopped. At Eden, too. The waters of the Deluge might have left it but a week before: so choked with slime and matted growth was the hideous swamp which bore that name" (MC, p. 377).

"The thunder rolled, the lightning flashed; the rain poured down like Heaven's wrath" (MC, p. 645).

"Sir Barnet and Lady Skettles, very good people, resided in a pretty villa at Fulham, on the banks of the Thames; which . . . had its little inconveniences . . . among which may be enumerated the occasional appearance of the river in the drawing-room, and the contemporaneous disappearance of the lawn and shrubbery" (D & S, p. 341).

"The obdurate bark [of the tree] was knotted and overlapped like the hide of a rhinoceros or some kindred monster of the ancient days before the Flood" (D&S, p. 380).

"There was a black barge, or some other kind of superannuated boat, not far off, high and dry on the ground" (DC, p. 29).

"Did you give your son the name of Ham, because you lived in a sort of Ark?" (David, DC, p. 32).

"Chatham . . . is a mere dream of chalk, and drawbridges, and mastless ships in a muddy river, roofed like Noah's arks" (DC, p. 183).

"The waters are out in Lincolnshire. An arch of the bridge in the park has been sapped and sopped away. An adjacent low-lying ground, for half a mile in breadth, is a stagnant river, with melancholy trees for islands in it, and a surface punctured all over, all day long, with falling rain. . . . The weather, for many a day and night, has been so wet that the trees seem wet through" (BH, p. 8).

"What follows? That the country is shipwrecked, lost, and gone to pieces" (BH, p. 161).

". . . the whole framework of society . . . receiving tremendous cracks in consequence of people . . . getting out of the station unto which they are called . . . and so obliterating the landmarks, and opening the floodgates, and all the rest of it." (BH, p. 397).

Peepy "brought down Noah with him (out of an ark I had given him before we went to church)" (Esther, BH, pp. 423-24).

"England has been some weeks in the dismal strait of having

no pilot . . . to weather the storm; and the marvellous part of the matter is, that England has not appeared to care very much about it, but has gone on eating and drinking and marrying and giving in marriage, as the old world did in the days before the flood" (BH, p. 532).

"Then upon my honour . . . the floodgates of society are burst open, and the waters have—a—obliterated the landmarks of the framework of the cohesion by which things are held together" (Sir Leicester, BH, pp. 570-71).

"Lord Decimus Tite Barnacle. . . . was always yet to be told that it behoved the Pilot of the ship to do anything but prosper in the private loaf and fish trade ashore, the crew being able, by dint of hard pumping, to keep the ship above water without him" (LD, p. 405).

"Seen from these solitudes . . . the ascending Night came up the mountain like a rising water. When it at last rose to the walls of the convent of the Great Saint Bernard, it was as if that weather-beaten structure were another Ark, and floated on the shadowy waves" (LD, p. 432).

"There was a smell within [the convent] . . . like the smell of a menagerie of wild animals" (LD, pp. 433-34).

"What private solicitude could rear itself against the deluge of the Year One of Liberty—the deluge rising from below, not falling from above, and with the windows of Heaven shut, not opened" (TTC, p. 259).

"By the light of the torches, we saw the black Hulk lying out a little way from the mud of the shore, like a wicked Noah's ark" (GE, p. 36).

"In my fancy, I saw the boat with its convict crew waiting for them at the slime-washed stairs . . . again saw the wicked Noah's ark lying out on the black water" (GE, p. 217).

"That's gas . . . coming out of a bit of a forest that's been under the mud that was under the water in the days of Noah's Ark" (Charley Hexam, OMF, p. 28).

"But on the way down they had stopped at a toy-shop, and had bought that novel charger . . . and also a Noah's ark" (OMF, p. 326).

"At the Children's Hospital, the gallant steed, the Noah's ark . . . were made as welcome as their child-owner" (OMF, p. 328).

Johnny watches "the appearance on his own little platform in pairs, of All Creation on its way into his own particular ark" (OMF, p. 329).

"O the wonderful Noah's Ark! It was not found seaworthy when put in a washing-tub, and the animals were crammed in at the roof, and needed to have their legs well shaken down before they could be got in. . . . Consider the noble fly, a size or two smaller than the elephant. . . . Consider the goose, whose feet were so small, and whose balance was so indifferent, that he usually tumbled forward, and knocked down all the animal creation. Consider Noah and his family, like idiotic tobacco-stoppers" ("A Christmas Tree," CS, pp. 7-8).

John Steadiman "was so taken with them on looking in at the toyshop while they were buying the child a cranky Noah's Ark" ("The Wreck of the Golden Mary," CS, p. 137).

"There's rather a run on Noah's Arks at present" (Caleb Plummer, *The Cricket on the Hearth*, p. 172).

". . . my head's so running on them Arks and things!" (Caleb Plummer, *The Cricket on the Hearth*, p. 173).

"There were various other samples of his handicraft besides Dolls, in Caleb Plummer's room. There were Noah's Arks, in which the Birds and Beasts were an uncommonly tight fit" (*The Cricket on the Hearth*, p. 184).

"All within this desolate creature is barren wilderness. . . . From every seed of evil in this boy, a field of ruin is grown that shall be gathered in . . . until regions are overspread with wickedness enough to raise the waters of another Deluge" (*The Haunted Man*, p. 378).

IV. *Babel*

". . . looking back at old St. Paul's looming through the smoke . . . [and] the Babel out of which it grew" (OCS, p. 116).

"Well! you come from an old country: from a country, sir, that has piled up golden calves as high as Babel, and worshipped 'em for ages" (General Choke, MC, p. 349).

"Everywhere were bridges that led nowhere; thoroughfares that were wholly impassable; Babel towers of chimneys, wanting half their height" (D&S, pp. 62-63).

"In an office that might have been on the ground-floor of the Tower of Babel, it was so massively constructed, we were presented to our old schoolmaster" (DC, p. 849).

". . . red-hot iron, white-hot iron, cold-black iron; an iron taste, an iron smell, and a Babel of iron sounds" (BH, p. 846).

"Hindoos, Russians, Chinese, Spaniards, Portuguese, Englishmen, Frenchmen, Genoese, Neapolitans, Venetians, Greeks, Turks, descendants from all the builders of Babel, come to trade at Marseilles" (LD, p. 1).

Coketown's "factories . . . their tall chimneys rising up into the air like competing Towers of Babel" (HT, p. 88).

"Unbelieving Philosophers who were remodelling the world with words, and making card-towers of Babel" (TTC, p. 100).

V. *Judgment Day*

The clock "did not mark the flight of every moment with a gentle stroke . . . but measured it with one sledgehammer beat, as

173

if its business were . . . remorselessly to clear a path before the Day of Judgment" (MHC, p. 107).

In Jonas Chuzzlewit's dream, "a terrible figure started out from the throng, and cried out that it was the Last Day for all the world" (MC, p. 271).

Miss Norris "had a novel way of combining [her] acquirements and bringing them to bear on any subject from Millinery to the Millennium, both inclusive" (MC, p. 288).

"I have the honour to attend Court regularly. With my documents. I expect a judgment. Shortly. On the Day of Judgment" (Miss Flite, BH, p. 33).

"My father expected a Judgment. . . . My brother. My sister. They all expected a Judgment. The same that I expect" (Miss Flite, BH, p. 498).

"My physician, Mr. Woodcourt, my dear, who was so exceedingly attentive to me. Though his services were rendered quite gratuitously. Until the Day of Judgment. I mean the judgment that will dissolve the spell upon me of the Mace and Seal" (Miss Flite, BH, p. 500).

"If we could only come to a Millennium, or something of that sort, I for one might have the pleasure of knowing a number of charming and talented persons from whom I am at present excluded" (Mrs. Merdle, LD, p. 292).

"Not drawin' nigh to folk, wi' kindness and patience . . . will never do 't till the' Sun turns t' ice . . . till God's work is onmade" (Stephen Blackpool, HT, p. 151).

"If a Day of Judgment had only been ascertained to be a dress day, everybody there would have been eternally correct" (TTC, p. 101).

"Seven faces of prisoners . . . all scared, all lost, all wandering and amazed, as if the Last Day were come . . . Other seven faces there were, carried higher, seven dead faces, whose drooping eyelids and half-seen eyes awaited the Last Day" (TTC, pp. 209-10).

"The world is drawing to an end, and the sun will never rise any more" (Mr. Rarx, "The Wreck of the Golden Mary," CS, p. 146).

VI. *Wilderness*

". . . in this wilderness of London. . . ."
"Wilderness! Yes it is, it is. Good! It *is* a wilderness. . . . It was a wilderness to me once" (Nicholas and Mr. Cheeryble, NN, p. 450).

"Between the Golden Key and the Black Lion there lay a wilderness of streets" (BR, p. 604).

"Mr. Richard Swiveller wending homewards from the Wilderness (for such was the appropriate name of Quilp's choice retreat) . . ." (OCS, p. 171).

"At last, [Quilp] travelled back to the Wilderness, which was within rifle-shot of his bachelor retreat" (OCS, pp. 380-81).

"Miss Sally Brass . . . would have borne the discomforts of the Wilderness with a very ill grace" (OCS, p. 382).

"It was ten o'clock at night before the amiable Sally supported her beloved and loving brother from the Wilderness" (OCS, p. 384).

"A day or two after the Quilp tea-party at the Wilderness. . ." (OCS, p. 414).

"There were steeples, towers, belfries, shining vanes, and masts of ships: a very forest. Gables, housetops, garret-windows, wilderness upon wilderness" (MC, p. 130).

"And now it was Martin's turn . . . to listen through the long,

long nights, to every sound in the gloomy wilderness" (MC, p. 523).

"So Florence lived in her wilderness of a home" (D&S, p. 320).

"She dreamed of seeking her father in wildernesses" (D&S, p. 508).

"She thought of the only other time she had been lost in the wilderness of London" (D&S, p. 667).

"I looked in all directions, as far as I could stare over the wilderness, and away at the sea" (DC, p. 29).

"Towards London, a lurid glare overhung the whole dark waste" (BH, p. 429).

"It is a moonlight night . . . over the great wilderness of London" (BH, p. 662).

"Not only is it a still night on dusty high-roads and on hill summits . . . but even on this stranger's wilderness of London there is some rest" (BH, p. 663).

"He had but glanced away at the piles of roofs and chimneys . . . and at the wilderness of masts on the river, and the wilderness of steeples on the shore" (LD, p. 79).

". . . the wilderness patched with unfruitful gardens and pimpled with eruptive summer-houses . . ." (LD, p. 144).

Clennam "could not have felt more depressed and cast away if he had been in a wilderness" (LD, p. 161).

"Wildernesses of corner houses . . . horrors that came into existence under some wrong-headed person in some wrong-headed time, still demanding the blind admiration of all ensuing generations and determined to do so until they tumbled down" (LD, p. 324).

". . . the secrets of the river, as it rolled its turbid tide between two frowning wildernesses of secrets, extending, thick and dense, for many miles" (LD, p. 543).

"The savage herdsmen and the fierce-looking peasants . . . left the wilderness blank" (LD, p. 637).

"What have you done, O father, what have you done, with the garden that should have bloomed once, in this great wilderness here?" (Louisa, HT, p. 216).

"Waste forces within him, and a desert all around, this man . . . saw, for a moment, lying in the wilderness before him, a mirage of honourable ambition" (TTC, p. 85).

"What is [France] but a wilderness of misery and ruin" (Charles Evremonde, TTC, p. 118).

"Now that we were out upon the dismal wilderness . . ." (GE, p. 30).

"In a by-yard, there was a wilderness of empty casks" (GE, p. 58).

"It was quite a wilderness" (GE, p. 83).

"By the wilderness of casks that I had walked on long ago . . . I made my way to the ruined garden" (GE, pp. 379-80).

"The back of [the Six Jolly Fellowship-Porters] . . . stood at the bottom of a wilderness of court and alley: which wilderness pressed so hard and close upon the Six Jolly Fellowship-Porters as to leave the hostelry not an inch of ground beyond its door" (OMF, p. 61).

"The night was black and shrill, the river-side wilderness was melancholy" (OMF, p. 70).

"A Dismal Swamp" (Chapter title, OMF, p. 209).

"In such a Dismal Swamp does the new house stand" (OMF, p. 212).

"A few boxes of humble flowers and evergreens completed [Mr. Riah's] garden; and the encompassing wilderness of dowager old chimneys twirled their cowls and fluttered their smoke" (OMF, p. 279).

"All within this desolate creature is barren wilderness. All within the man bereft of what you have resigned, is the same barren wilderness" (*The Haunted Man*, p. 378).

VII. *Maze*

Oliver "soon became involved in a maze of the mean and dirty streets which abound in that close and densely-populated quarter" (OT, p. 135).

"To reach [Jacob's Island] the visitor has to penetrate through a maze of close, narrow, and muddy streets" (OT, p. 381).

"A kind of resigned distraction came over the stranger as he trod these devious mazes" (MC, p. 127).

Bleak House is "one of those delightfully irregular houses where you go up and down steps out of one room into another, and where you come upon more rooms when you think you have seen all there are, and where there is a bountiful provision of little halls and passages" (BH, p. 65).

"At last they came into a maze of dust, where a quantity of people were tumbling over one another, and where there was such a confusion of unaccountable shapes of beams, bulkheads, brick walls, ropes, and rollers . . . that they seemed to have got on the wrong side of the pattern of the universe. . . . [Fanny] conducted her to a more open part of the maze" (LD, p. 234).

". . . never-resting wreaths and mazes of mist wandered about, hunted by a moaning wind" (LD, p. 432).

"I was lost in the mazes of my future fortunes" (GE, p. 133).

A Concordance for Dickens's Mythology

VIII. *Labyrinth*

"Never were such labyrinths of uncarpeted passages . . . as are collected together between the four walls of the Great White Horse at Ipswich" (PP, p. 303).

"And now he approached the great city . . . reddening the sluggish air with a deep dull light, that told of labyrinths of public ways and shops, and swarms of busy people" (BR, p. 26).

"Before they had penetrated very far into the labyrinth of men's abodes . . ." (OCS, p. 114).

"Todgers's was in a labyrinth, whereof the mystery was known but to a chosen few" (MC, p. 127).

"Tiers upon tiers of vessels, scores of masts, labyrinths of tackle . . ." (MC, p. 622).

"There was a labyrinth of scaffolding raised all round the house from the basement to the roof" (D&S, p. 404).

"The church Walter had chosen for the purpose, was a mouldy old church in a yard, hemmed in by a labyrinth of back streets and courts" (D&S, p. 792).

Jack Maldon "sketched so many soldiers, and ladies' heads, over the Doctor's manuscript, that I often became involved in labyrinths of obscurity" (DC, pp. 523-24).

"He can't be expected to know much of such a labyrinth" (Richard Carstone, BH, p. 695).

"We rattled with great rapidity through such a labyrinth of streets, that I soon lost all idea where we were" (Esther, BH, p. 770).

"A labyrinth of grandeur. . . . A waste of unused passages and staircases. . . . Thus Chesney Wold" (BH, p. 875).

179

"Frederick . . . accepted every incident of the labyrinthian world in which he had got lost" (LD, p. 221).

Clennam "dived in among . . . the little streets . . . of which there is a labyrinth near Park Lane" (LD, p. 324).

Lord Decimus makes "howling labyrinths of sentences which he seemed to take for high roads" (LD, p. 408).

". . . a labyrinth of bare passages and pillared galleries" (LD, p. 464).

"Nobody knew that [Merdle] had any capacity . . . which had ever thrown, for any creature, the feeblest farthing-candle ray of light on any path . . . among the multiplicity of paths in the labyrinth trodden by the sons of Adam" (LD, p. 556).

"Without having been able closely to follow Mrs. Finching through this labyrinth, Little Dorrit understood its purpose" (LD, p. 820).

"In the hardestworking part of Coketown . . . at the heart of the labyrinth of narrow courts upon courts, and close streets upon streets . . . lived a certain Stephen Blackpool" (HT, p. 63).

INDEX

Art, 1, 7, 9-10, 27, 46, 49, 65, 67, 69, 71, 72, 74, 75-76, 77-78, 80-82, 84, 86, 98, 115, 117, 139
Austen, Jane, 108

Babel, 6, 25, 30, 58, *104-05*, 113, 116-17, 157, *158-60*, 162, *173*
Bachelors, 4, 17, 31, 33, 59, 61, 67, 98, 136-37, 138-39, 145
Benevolence, 3, 4, 9, 10-13, 14, 17, 19, 21, 23, 31, 33, 34, 49, 59, 61, 67, 97, 144, 158
Blake, William, 77, 102, 123
Brooke, G. L., 106
Butt, John, 75

Carlyle, Thomas, 73, 74
Change, 5, 6, 14, 35-36, 58-59, 60, 62, 65, 78, 84-85, 87, 90, 92, 94, 95, 97, 102-03, 105, 112, 114, 118-21, 127-29, 132, 136, 138, 140-42, 146, 150, 153-54, 158, 160
Chesterfield, 37
Christianity, 2, 17-22, 24-26, 28-30, 32-33, 35, 37-38, 39, 40, 55-58, 63, 71, 86-87, 93, 95, 99, 111-12, 116, 122, 152, 153, 158, 159
Class Society, 2, 27, 35, 36-37, 41, 90, 124, *127-29*, 133, 136, 138, 139, 140, 145, 152, 154-55
Collins, Wilkie, 6, 100, 154
Conrad, Joseph, 95
Creation, 6, 7, 23, 25, 27, 43-44, 60, 64, 86-90, 98-99, 101, 104, 118, 120-22, 125, 141, 154, 157, 160, *162-63*

Deluge, x, xi, 6, 7, 25-26, 40, 44-45, 67-68, 82, 86, 87, 89, 90-91, 95,

98-99, 104, *105-08*, 109, 111, 118, 119, 122-23, 125, 130, *141-44*, 154-55, 157-58, 160-61, 162, *169-73*
Dickens, Charles,
  Barnaby Rudge, 22, *35-40*, 119-20, 164, 175, 179
  Bleak House, 2, 3, 4, 17, 36, 61, 64, 69, 74, 76, *83-99*, 103, 108, 109, 119, 122, 158, 159, 163, 170-71, 173-74, 176, 178-79
  "Christmas Carol, A," 160
  "Christmas Tree, A," 172
  "Cricket on the Hearth, The," 172
  David Copperfield, 1, 2, 3, 4, 7, 9, 18, 25, 61, *63-82*, 92, 103, 117, 119, 126, 127, 128, 135, 137, 158, 159, 162, 167, 170, 173, 176, 179
  Dombey and Son, 3, 4, 17, *52-62*, 112, 134, 155, 158, 159, 167, 169-70, 173, 176, 179
  Great Expectations, 2, 4, 7, 33, 34, 36, 48, 85, 103, 108, 124, *125-37*, 138, 146, 168-69, 171, 177-78
  Hard Times, 2, 4, 63, 64, 76, 88, 108, *111-17*, 119, 128, 158, 159, 173-74, 177, 180
  "Haunted Man, The," 173, 178
  "Holly-Tree Inn, The," 111, 112
  Household Words, 116, 127
  Little Dorrit, 2, 4, 12, 83, 84, 88, *99-110*, 114, 119, 154, 159, 163, 167-68, 171, 173-74, 176-77, 178
  Martin Chuzzlewit, 4, *40-52*, 61, 76, 77, 117, 158, 162, 164, 169, 173-76, 178, 179
  Master Humphrey's Clock, 28, 29, 173-74

Index